Elite • 268

Roman Cavalry Helmets

M.C. BISHOP

ILLUSTRATED BY GIUSEPPE RAVA

Series editor Nick Reynolds

OSPREY PUBLISHING
Bloomsbury Publishing Plc
Kemp House, Chawley Park, Cumnor Hill, Oxford OX2 9PH, UK
Bloomsbury Publishing Ireland Limited,
29 Earlsfort Terrace, Dublin 2, D02 AY28, Ireland
Bloomsbury Publishing Inc.
1359 Broadway, 12th Floor, New York, NY 10018, USA
E-mail: info@ospreypublishing.com
www.ospreypublishing.com

OSPREY is a trademark of Osprey Publishing Ltd

First published in Great Britain in 2026

A catalogue record for this book is available from the British Library.

ISBN: PB 9781472871169; eBook 9781472871176;
ePDF 9781472871145; XML 9781472871152

26 27 28 29 30 10 9 8 7 6 5 4 3 2 1

Index by Richard Munro
Typeset by Lumina Datamatics Ltd
Printed and bound in India by Repro India Ltd.

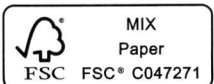

Osprey Publishing supports the Woodland Trust, the UK's leading woodland
conservation charity.

To find out more about our authors and books visit
www.ospreypublishing.com. Here you will find extracts, author
interviews, details of forthcoming events and the option to
sign up for our newsletter.

For product safety related questions contact productsafety@bloomsbury.com

Acknowledgements

As the companion volume to Elite 266, *Roman Infantry Helmets*, many of
the same people are owed thanks. My late friend and colleague, Dr Jon
Coulston, was a huge influence on what follows, as a result of our
discussions on the subject of Roman helmets over the years, not least their
depiction on Trajan's Column and elsewhere. Similarly, conversations with
the late Peter Connolly over the protection offered by Roman headgear
were always stimulating and productive. As ever, Dr David Sim was an
invaluable source of information on the subject of manufacturing helmets,
while Alan Larsen was very informative (over a pint) in the aftermath of the
Turma! Hadrian's Cavalry event in 2017. Sue Willets of the Joint Library of
the Hellenic and Roman Societies went out of her way to supply a badly
needed reference; in fact, the importance of that library to everything I
have written has been incalculable. Finally, I should once again like to thank
my editor, Nick Reynolds, for his patience and understanding.

Artist's note

Readers may care to note that the original paintings from which the colour
plates in this book were prepared are available for private sale.
All reproduction copyright whatsoever is retained by the publishers.
All enquiries should be addressed to:

info@g-rava.it

The publishers regret that they can enter into no correspondence upon
this matter.

Title-page illustration: An unprovenanced Weyler-type battle helmet now
in a private collection. The bowl is ferrous with stylized locks of hair and a
decorated copper-alloy fronton and ear guards, while the cheek pieces
have embossed copper-alloy sheaths. (© Trimontium Trust)

CONTENTS

ROMAN CAVALRY HELMETS

INTRODUCTION

Attempting to summarize the development of Roman cavalry helmets in one short volume is no easier than it is for infantry helmets, albeit not always for the same reasons. There is an inevitable overlap in some areas with the companion volume to this (Bishop 2025), when considering cavalry helmets. Sometimes, the same sources are just as relevant. Repetition has been kept to a minimum in what follows, but some facts will inevitably reoccur here.

By the same token, misunderstandings of Roman cavalry helmets abound and attempts to highlight and correct these have to be made. Helmets with any hint of decoration are all too frequently categorized as 'parade' equipment (implying they would not be worn in battle) or 'officer's' headgear, without any substantiating proof (see p.44). The predilection of the regular auxiliary cavalry trooper for, at times, extreme levels of decoration should never be underestimated, however, not least as a statement of conspicuous consumption over his less-well-paid infantry counterpart, but also to impress an enemy.

The publication in 1983 of a Roman cavalry helmet found with a cremation burial in a tumulus at Weyler, in the Belgian province of Luxembourg (not to be confused with the neighbouring country of the same name), began one of the more bizarre tales of helmet nomenclature (Fairon & Moreau-Maréchal 1983). Referring to the 'casque de Weiler' in the pages of the journal *Germania*, the paper's title actually referred to the 'casque de Weyler'. Hence, this helmet form has ever since tended to be referred to as the 'Weiler type'. In what follows, however, the term 'Weyler type' will be employed for the sake of both authenticity and sanity.

Cavalry battle helmet from a burial at Weyler. (Photo © Karwansaray Publishers)

Battle helmet from the Tell 'Umm Hōrān burial near Nawa in crushed condition, as found. (Photo © J.C.N. Coulston)

This is far from the only problematic area of Roman cavalry helmet nomenclature. A general grouping of 'Weiler/Guisborough' was defined and a comparison made with cavalry helmets depicted on tombstones (Waurick 1988b: 341–45). At the same time, face-mask helmets (*Gesichtshelme*) were included as a separate category. This continental classification of cavalry helmets was largely ignored by H. Russell Robinson, however, who distinguished between his Auxiliary Cavalry and Cavalry Sports types (1975: 89–135). Although his Auxiliary Cavalry types A to C were straightforward enough, the inclusion of the Niederbieber helmet and its various contemporary parallels was to cause difficulties once it was realized that these were in fact infantry helmets. Fischer's subsequent identification of their true nature then left a gap for cavalry battle helmets of the 2nd and 3rd centuries AD, which he proceeded to fill with first his pseudo-Attic and then pseudo-Corinthian types of helmet (Fischer 2018; 2019: 181–85), which Robinson (1975: 131–35) had confusingly included among his Cavalry Sports types (H to J).

Thus, use of Robinson's classification of Principate cavalry helmets, although still widespread, is unhelpful and will largely be avoided here. As with the companion volume on infantry helmets (Bishop 2025: 5), Fischer's system of helmet classification will broadly be followed.

Cavalry helmets, just like those of the infantry, could sustain three distinct types of damage. Pre-depositional damage refers to harm that occurred before the helmet was discarded, such as battle damage that could be repaired, component failure, or even misuse. Peri-depositional damage includes irreversible damage, such as severe battle damage, discarded items not accepted for recycling, or incidents during the helmet's entry into the archaeological record – for example, being crushed beneath rubble. Post-depositional damage would have happened after the helmet has been discarded and might include corrosion or disturbances caused by environmental or human activity. A helmet recovered from the archaeological record can show evidence of one or more of these types of damage, but one thing seems certain: it is very unlikely to have been lost accidentally.

ORIGINS

Just as with infantry helmets, frustratingly little is known about early Roman cavalry headgear. No examples have been excavated that can be said to be unequivocally 'Roman', rather than Italian (at a time when Rome was just one of many comparable states on the Italian peninsula). This paucity of data is a result of the way in which helmets were deposited in the archaeological record. In the early stages of Rome's development, only the rich could afford to leave items of equipment as grave goods. It was not until the Principate that the combination of a standing army and a developed recycling system meant comparatively large amounts of material came to be discarded, far outweighing the volume of material lost on battlefield sites, for example.

Artefactual evidence is not the only source of information, however. A number of Samnite tomb frescoes depict mounted warriors returning from battle with captured items of enemy clothing. As cavalry at this time were inevitably formed from the wealthy elites who could afford the possession and maintenance of a horse, these men would seem to merit consideration here. On an example from Nola (Italy), now lost, the warrior is shown wearing a muscled copper-alloy cuirass and a form of the Attic helmet in the same material with side plumes. This type of helmet was adopted

Samnite warrior wearing an Attic helmet, from a 4th-century BC fresco in a tomb in Nola. (Shonagon/Wikimedia/Public Domain)

on the Italian peninsula via the Greek presence in Magna Graecia.

Literary evidence can also occasionally be of assistance. The Roman facility for adopting and adapting the technologies and methodologies of other peoples was commented upon by Arrian (the Roman Army commander and historian Flavius Arrianus):

> Indeed, if the Romans deserve praise for any quality, it is for not loving solely their own customs and heritage, but rather for choosing the best practices from everywhere and making them their own. Thus, you may observe that some weapons, although borrowed from others, are now called 'Roman' because the Romans have mastered their use. (Arrian, *Tēchne Taktikē* 33.2–3, tr. author)

The first true cavalry helmet of the Roman Army may in fact have been the same Montefortino type used by infantry but, if this was indeed so, it will remain difficult to prove this unless an inscribed example comes to light. So far, despite hundreds of examples being known, this has not occurred, perhaps due to literacy levels in early Roman armies, or simply because the 'epigraphic habit' did not catch on with Regal and Early Republican military equipment in the same way that it did with that of the Principate and later.

Unlike infantry helmets, the prototypes for Roman cavalry helmets before the Dominate were seldom those used by enemies or allies. The separate and highly individualistic development strands, particularly under the Principate, are as intriguing as they are informative about the status and self-image of Roman cavalrymen.

Montefortino helmet from Cerro de la Horca, Algeciras (Spain). (Jerónimo Roure Pérez/ Wikimedia/CC BY-SA 4.0)

TERMINOLOGY

As has been noted for infantry helmets (Bishop 2025: 7–8), two particular Latin words are to be found referring to helmets: *cassis* and *galea*. Isidore of Seville, the 6th/7th-century AD lexicographer, noted: 'The helmet [*cassis*] is of sheet metal or leather [*galea*], leather caps being called *galeri*. However, the *cassis* was so termed by the Etruscans; for they called the helmet *cassis*, I believe, from 'head' [*caput*]' (Isidore, *Etymologiae* 18.14, tr. author).

The true contrast between the two terms is now lost, and only further muddied by historians like Tacitus, using the terms for artistic effect. The interchangeability of *cassis* and *galea* in his writing can be illustrated in a passage describing the Germans: 'A few only have body armour, and just one or two here and there a *cassis* or *galea*' (Tacitus, *Germania* 6, tr. Church & Brodribb, amended author).

The words were similarly confused by Vegetius. Nor does the type of metal used to manufacture a helmet – copper alloy or ferrous metal (normally steel) – provide a convincing reason to suspect that *cassis* represented one type and *galea* the other. Similarly, there is no evidence that infantry or cavalry helmets were referred to by one or other term.

REPUBLICAN CAVALRY HELMETS

We are fortunate to possess the observations of a contemporary Greek, with knowledge of both Greek and Republican Roman cavalry equipment: 'The cavalry's equipment today is similar to that of the Greeks, but in the past, they did not initially wear breastplates. Instead, they fought wearing only a belt, which made them agile and effective for quickly dismounting and remounting their horses, but left them vulnerable in close combat since they fought unarmoured' (Polybios, *Histories* 6.25.3).

The earliest forms of Roman cavalry helmet are unknown. Comparison with other contemporary warriors in Italy suggest that the Attic type of helmet was one of those used by cavalry. The fresco from a 4th-century BC tomb in Nola depicts a Samnite horseman wearing an Attic helmet, which, from its colour, was made of copper alloy. The question as to whether Roman equipment at the time mimicked Samnite remains moot, however.

HISTORY

The Montefortino type of helmet probably featured at some point as Roman cavalry headgear, because they were certainly used by the Etruscans for this purpose. A relief on an alabaster funerary urn from Volterra (Italy), and dated to the 1st century BC (Taylor 2017: 289), depicts an Etruscan cavalryman bidding farewell to his wife. Standing between his horse and his spouse, he holds a spear and wears mail body armour over *pteryges*, and on his head is a readily recognizable Montefortino helmet (albeit, true to Hellenistic artistic practices, omitting the cheek piece, where one should be visible, in order to emphasize his face). Given the likely date in the 1st century BC, this presumably represents a member of the allied cavalry (who would have been equipped in the same way as the Roman citizen cavalry). Like the *gladius Hispaniensis* (Bishop 2016: 10), the Montefortino helmet was well-suited to use by both infantry and cavalry. The large cheek pieces and small neck guard have much in common with cavalry helmets under the Principate, as will become apparent.

One important clue to Late Republican cavalry headgear comes from the so-called Altar of Domitius Ahenobarbus from Rome (Italy). Among various military figures, including legionaries and an officer, there is a cavalryman with what appears to be a Boeotian helmet. This resonates with what Polybios wrote about 'equipment similar to that of the Greeks' (by which he presumably meant Hellenistic Greeks or Macedonians). The Altar of Domitius Ahenobarbus is generally thought to date to the late 2nd century BC, coinciding with the later years of Polybios' life (his *Histories* ran up to 146 BC), with his death thought to have occurred around 118 BC at the age of 82 (Lucian of Samosata, *Macrobioi* 24).

By the end of the 2nd century BC, the design of Boeotian helmets was over 200 years old. The type had in fact been recommended to cavalrymen by Xenophon in the 4th century BC: 'We consider the Boeotian-made helmet to be the best, for it provides the greatest coverage for all parts, extending beyond the cuirass while not obstructing vision' (Xenophon, *Peri hippikēs* 12.3).

No Boeotian helmets have been recovered from Roman Republican contexts, in marked contrast to infantry helmets of the period. An example from the Tigris River, now in the Ashmolean Museum in Oxford (England),

probably dates to the Hellenistic era. The form supposedly originated with the *petasos* Illyrian sun hat. By the Roman period, it is thought to have developed a more conical bowl, possibly influenced by the Montefortino type of infantry helmet, and it could be this that can be seen being worn with a horsehair crest on the so-called Altar of Domitius Ahenobarbus.

There is another possibility, however, which is that the helmet depicted on the monument is in fact a Gallic derivative of the Boeotian helmet, the so-called Western Celtic form, represented by examples from Forêt de Rouvray and Forêt de Louviers (both France; Schaaff 1988: Abb.29 33). These have a similar creases in the brim of the helmet to that shown on the relief, but crucially also rise to a point where a crest could be attached. Finding such a helmet in an indisputable Roman context might help solve this puzzle.

DESCRIPTION

Montefortino helmets in Roman service were made of copper alloy, almost invariably a bronze during the Republican period. Derived from Gallic types, which were then adopted by the Etruscans, this type of helmet was furnished with a sub-spherical, oval bowl that rose to the top (*apex*), where an integral crest knob was situated. The small neck guard was a continuation of the thickened helmet brim to the rear. Although omitted from the Volterra relief, cheek pieces were flat and had two frontal scalloped indentations. They were hinged to the bowl at the side by means of a hinge plate fixed to the interior of the bowl with one or two rivets. By the Late Republican period, the three-point system of securing the helmet to a soldier's head had been adopted, with tie rings in the centre underside of the neck guard and in the lower part of the interior of each cheek piece.

The form of the Boeotian helmet was composed of a copper-alloy bowl and a broad brim, turned down at the sides and back, with two creases on either side emulating the brim of the hat after which it was modelled.

Hellenistic Boeotian helmet found in the Tigris River. (Gts-tg/Wikimedia/ CC BY-SA 4.0)

The rear two creases defined a neck guard, while the front two likewise delineate a brow guard. In Macedonian use, this type of helmet did not employ cheek pieces, as is clear from the late-4th-century BC Alexander Sarcophagus. The relief of the cavalryman on the Altar is posed so that it is impossible to tell whether there is a cheek piece on the helmet. An example in Larissa museum has small holes in the bottom of each of four creases, perhaps to secure a lining, or even provide a means of securing the helmet to the wearer's head.

The Western Celtic helmet type clearly resembles the Boeotian in some ways, enough to suggest that it was modelled on the Greek type. In that respect, it still meets Polybios' comment that contemporary Roman cavalry equipment 'is similar to that of the Greeks'. Each has a bulbous bowl, rising to a pointed apex topped by a crest knob, and above a circumferential ridge, below which is the downturned brim, which has creases similar to the Boeotian helmet. It is finished with hinged, bicuspid cheek pieces.

VARIANTS

Although Robinson identified four basic types of Montefortino helmet (1975: 17–18), Paddock (1993: 508–20) later refined this to 12 forms in four groups (although his four groups, based on the form of the crest knob, did not match those of Robinson). Of those 12, nine, possibly ten, were in his opinion Republican in date. Only one type of what Paddock recorded as Republican Montefortino helmets actually has surviving cheek pieces.

PADDOCK'S REPUBLICAN MONTEFORTINO HELMET TYPES			
Type	Date	Bowl	Cheek pieces
VI	3rd/2nd century BC	high conical bowl with a truncated, conical, decorated crest knob; a deep, flattened neck guard; moderately thick rim with a narrow cable motif with six rows of fluting (with two or more rows of triangles)	thick cheek pieces with an exaggerated bicuspid form; hinges attached with two rivets
VII	3rd/2nd century BC	moderately straight-sided conical bowl topped by a truncated, conical, decorated crest knob; a short neck guard; thinner rim and reduced cable motif with simple file cuts (with two or more rows of triangles)	no cheek pieces survive; hinges attached with two rivets
VIII	2nd/1st century BC	bulbous bowl with near-vertical sides and a hemispherical, conical or truncated plain conical crest knob; deep sloping or flattened neck guard; rim that is still thickened but less so than before, with slight cabling at the front of the rim but not on the neck guard	no cheek pieces survive; hinges attached with two rivets
IX	2nd/1st century BC	finish is poor and has a high bulbous bowl with near-vertical sides; plain crest knob is discoid or a truncated cone; a moderately deep, sloping or flattened neck guard; rim is still thickened but undecorated	no cheek pieces survive; hinges attached with single rivet
X	Undated	moderately high, slightly bulbous, hemispherical bowl with a crest knob that is now separate and riveted to the bowl; short, sloping neck guard with plain moulding on its edge and is delineated by two incised lines; rim is still thickened but now undecorated	no cheek pieces survive; hinges usually attached with two rivets

With no Roman examples of the Boeotian helmet surviving, the Hellenistic example fashioned from copper alloy found in the Tigris River (Waurick 1988a: 159) will suffice to illustrate what a Roman one might have been like. It was found in 1854 near Tille (Turkey) in the Tigris and ultimately acquired by the Ashmolean Museum. The brim itself is pierced by a pair of holes on the right-hand side, punched through from the inside, but these are not matched on the other side. It does not share the pairs of holes at the edge of the brim on either side of an example from Larissa (Greece), nor the series of holes around the edge of the neck guard of the Ruse helmet (Stoyanov *et al.* 2023). The Tigris bowl is damaged near the apex and on the left-hand side (it was reportedly retrieved accidentally with a boathook).

The bowl is notable for imitating the brim of a hat and doing so in such a way that it serves the functions of brow guard, cheek pieces and neck guard without the need for any additional components. These sections are delineated by stylized folds in the brim (similar details can be made out on the depiction of the so-called Altar of Domitius Ahenobarbus). There is no crest knob of the sort that would be expected of the helmet depicted on the Roman monument.

Two examples of Western Celtic helmets come from Forêt de Rouvray and Forêt de Louviers. Both retain their cheek pieces and the former still has its crest knob, so they merit consideration here as an alternative to the pure Boeotian form with regard to what is depicted on the Altar relief.

The Forêt de Rouvray helmet

The ferrous helmet from Forêt de Rouvray was found in an isolated burial, along with a sheathed sword, suspension rings and a torc. The tomb was broadly dated to the second to third quarters of the 1st century BC (Pernet 2010: 258–59 & pl.235), and so the helmet would match the suggested dating for the so-called Altar of Domitius Ahenobarbus. The helmet not only has both cheek pieces, but also possesses both tie rings towards the bottom rear of each cheek piece. A protruding, triangular-sectioned ridge running around the base of the bowl and above the brim may have acted in a similar manner to the brow guard on Roman infantry helmets under the Principate. The helmet measures 249mm front to back and is 240mm high without cheek pieces, and 387mm with them.

The helmet has not been fully published (Schaaff 1988: 307–08), but its origins as a derivative of the Boeotian helmet are clear. As no examples of Boeotian helmets with a pointed apex have been found and because this type has that feature and (in this case) a crest holder on top, it is not unreasonable to assume that this may indeed be the helmet type represented on the Altar.

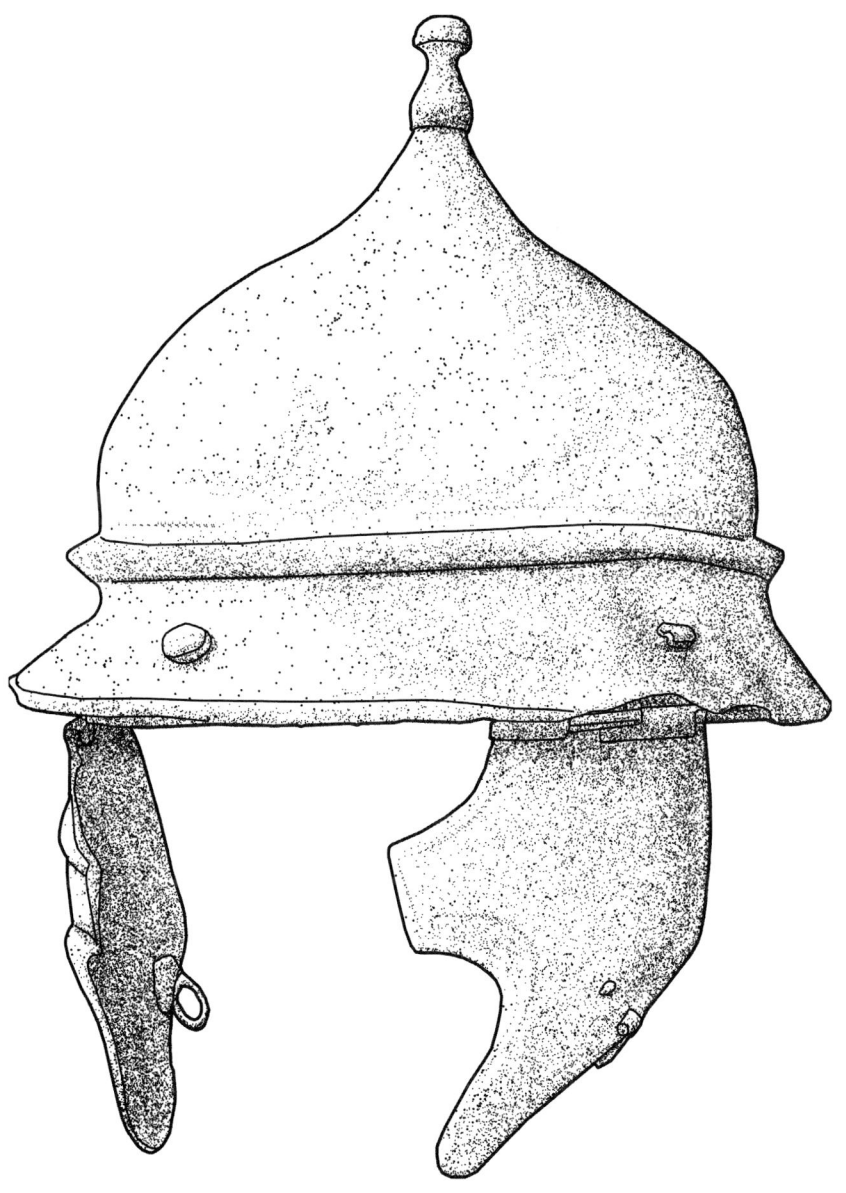

Western Celtic helmet from Forêt de Rouvray, a derivative of the Boeotian type. (Drawing © M.C. Bishop)

PRINCIPATE CAVALRY HELMETS

Silver stater from Velia in Lucania (Italy) depicting Athena wearing an Attic helmet, dating from 400–365 BC. (cgb. fr/Wikimedia/CC BY-SA 3.0 Unported)

It was during the Principate that cavalry helmet development bifurcated into two distinct strands, one for battle helmets and the other for face-mask or 'sports' helmets. Among surviving helmets, an unprovenanced Weisenau/ Imperial-Gallic helmet from the Guttmann collection (Fischer 2019: 177), which features a face mask hinged to it at the front of the rim, appears to coincide with this bifurcation. The face mask was designed to fit within the cheek pieces, which were enlarged to cover the ear recesses in the helmet bowl and bore an idealized, moulded representation of the wearer's ear, something that would become familiar on subsequent developments of cavalry helmets. A similar face mask was found at the Kalkriese (Germany) battlefield site, generally assumed to be associated with the Varus disaster of AD 9, conveniently supplying a *terminus ante quem* for the introduction of such hybrid helmets (which may very well have originated as field modifications).

The development of a fashion for accurate portrayals of deceased Roman soldiers on their tombstones developed in the Early Principate. With their pay substantially above that of auxiliary infantrymen and almost on a par with legionaries, cavalrymen proved to be willing customers for this new trend. Some superb examples provide very clear representations of cavalry battle helmets, but depictions of 'sports' helmets are much rarer and, in some cases, questionable.

Although face-mask helmets are sometimes suggested as being depicted worn on cavalry tombstones, as in the case of Flavinus of *ala Petriana* from Hexham (England; Robinson & Embleton 1978: 3–5), there is in fact no clear evidence to support it. On the contrary, the presence of cheek pieces on such sculptural reliefs can be taken as evidence against such a hypothesis, by dint of the fact that only one known face-mask helmet features mock cheek pieces (see p.59). There are some occurrences of face-mask helmets in the iconographic record – such as a *congeries armorum* (collection of military equipment) frieze from Arles (France) – but none indisputably showing them actually in use.

In what follows (for the sake of clarity), the battle helmets of the Early, High and Late Principate have been separated from the face-mask helmets of the entire Principate. It might be as well to recall here that there could

Congeries armorum frieze from Arles depicting military equipment, including a helmet with a face mask. (francia2010/ Flickr/CC BY-SA 2.0)

be a considerable amount of time between the occasion when a helmet was manufactured, when it saw service, and when it was finally discarded and entered the archaeological record. A lingering suspicion that many of the helmets deposited during the upheavals of the 3rd century AD may in fact date back to the latter part of the 2nd century could well be justified. At the same time, typologies should not be allowed to mask the possibility of contemporaneity (perhaps regional) among different types of helmets. Thus the pseudo-Attic types may very well have overlapped with the pseudo-Corinthian, an assertion that the Worthing (England) helmet seems to support, and the Pfrondorf (Germany) helmet could well have been in use at the same time as the more traditional battle and two-part face-mask helmets.

Black-figure painting by Lysippides depicting Achilles with a Corinthian helmet pushed back on top of his head. (Photo ArchaiOptix/Wikimedia/ CC BY-SA 4.0 International)

HISTORY

As was the case with infantry helmets (Bishop 2025: 16), the Principate was a bountiful source of examples of Roman cavalry helmets, both near-intact and in component form, due to the way the mechanisms of archaeological deposition changed over time. Basing troops in permanently fortified sites with a system of maintenance and recycling was key to this (see p.48).

The same three broad phases of development can be discerned for cavalry helmets as for their infantry counterparts. These more or less correspond to what are nowadays known as the Early, High and Late Principate. These periods might further be loosely classified as Augustan to Trajanic (Early), Hadrianic to Commodan (High) and Severan to the beginning of the Dominate (Late).

Cheek piece from a Weyler-type battle helmet from the Waal River at IJzeren. (National Museum of Antiquities, Leiden/ CC BY-SA)

Detail of the relief from the Early Principate tombstone of the cavalryman Flavius Bassus of the *ala Afrorum* depicting him wearing a Weyler-type battle helmet. (Photo © M.C. Bishop)

The Early Principate

The aforementioned unprovenanced helmet originally from the Guttmann collection has been suggested as the first identifiable cavalry helmet of the Early Principate, because it not only has cheek pieces that cover the ear but also a hinged copper-alloy face mask of the type found at Kalkriese and associated with the aftermath of the disaster involving Varus' army in AD 9. Otherwise, the helmet bowl largely conforms to the typical ferrous Weisenau/Imperial-Gallic helmet of the time. It has reinforcing ribs across the occipital region at the back of the neck and half-moon-shaped reinforces on the neck guard just below that, as well as decorative bosses around the rivets on the bowl and cheek pieces. The only unusual details are separate appliqué copper-alloy 'eyebrows'.

The Weyler type of helmet was the first true cavalry helmet of the Principate, however, and there are a number of depictions surviving. The memorial to Flavius Bassus from Köln (Germany) is arguably one of the finest, with what appears to be a Weyler-type helmet (a variant of the type has even been named as a sub-type of the Weyler type proper: Fischer 2019: 178). The bowl is adorned with stylized curls, while there is a small neck guard, a cheek piece and a diadem or 'fronton' (a triangular addition at the front of the helmet, resembling a pediment, imitating Attic helmets of the past) above the wearer's face. Similar representations appear on the tombstones of C. Romanius and Silius from Mainz (Germany), and M. Aemilius Durises, Romanus and Longinus Biarta from Köln Most of these memorials date to the second half of the 1st century AD.

The High Principate

During the 2nd century AD, a new form of cavalry helmet began to be used. It was not one of what Robinson termed his Auxiliary Cavalry helmets, but – as Fischer has shown – the pseudo-Attic form. With all changes in equipment, it is unlikely that there was a sudden event, but rather a gradual introduction as older helmets were lost in combat or damaged beyond repair and scrapped. A number of examples of the pseudo-Attic type of helmet have been found, but the dating evidence for most of them is circumstantial. The Attic helmet was beloved of metropolitan artists depicting (their interpretation of) Roman headgear. A copper-alloy appliqué from the fort at Saalburg (Germany) depicts a cavalryman standing next to his horse and holding it by the bridle. He is clad in mail and wears his sword on a baldric on his right hip (so probably dates from the first half of the 2nd century AD), and is shown wearing what may be an Attic or pseudo-Attic helmet with a short fore-and-aft crest on the apex. Ironically, this popular impression of military equipment seems to have come to influence the real thing with the adoption of the pseudo-Attic type. Its similarities to the earlier Weyler type, such as the small neck guard, cheek pieces that cover the ear, and the fact that it originally incorporated an iron core, confirm its role as a cavalry helmet sheathing. A late form of the Weyler type was recovered from a tomb at Tell 'Umm Hōrān near Nawa (Syria; Helmet B), but this differed in being

Appliqué figurine from Saalburg depicting a cavalryman (wearing a pseudo-Attic battle helmet) from the High Principate with his horse. (Author's collection)

Coin of Probus showing the emperor wearing a stylized pseudo-Corinthian helmet (Münzkabinett Berlin Online Catalogue PD 1.0)

adorned with embossed figures, similar to those on the face-mask helmet found with it (Abdul-Hak 1954–55: 175–85).

The Late Principate

In Fischer's scheme of things, the pseudo-Attic cavalry helmet type was succeeded by the pseudo-Corinthian. One of his principal reasons for suggesting this was recognizing stylized depictions of the latter on some Roman emperor coin portraits from the 3rd century AD, beginning with Gallienus (Fischer 2019: 184). Hellenizing tendencies in Roman art had long favoured the human form over accurate representations of equipment. This was already evident on the helical frieze of Trajan's Column, on which helmets were shown as covering less of the face than was really the case, particularly by means of reducing the size of cheek pieces. The helmets on the coins identified by Fischer followed this tradition, compromising by showing emperors with partial pseudo-Corinthian helmets that left their portraits readily identifiable, for obvious reasons.

The Pfrondorf hybrid helmet. (Lindenschmit/Public Domain)

The ferrous core from a Weyler-type battle helmet excavated from the Kops Plateau at Nijmegen. (Collectie Valkhof Museum, Archeologisch Depot Gelderland/CC0)

Face-mask helmets

As is apparent from the Guttmann collection Weisenau/Imperial-Gallic-type helmet, the earliest face masks date to the beginning of the Early Principate and seem to have been paired with regular cavalry battle helmets and designed to fit beneath cheek pieces. These masks, typified by the example recovered from the battlefield site at Kalkriese, are androgynous and, unlike later examples, only cover the face in front of the ears. The next development seems to have been pairing full-face masks (complete with ears) with ferrous bowls similar to those used on Weyler-type battle helmets, which were then provided with textile covers. At this point, the helmets were not 'themed', but merely decorated. The logical next step would be the embossed ferrous and copper-alloy bowls familiar from the latter part of the 1st and early 2nd centuries AD, completing the divergence from battle helmets (which began once there was no longer provision for cheek pieces but only the centrally hinged mask). These then led to themed helmets employing iconography from the Trojan War (c.13th or 12th century BC), before evolution came full circle and the battle and face-mask helmets reunited with the Pfrondorf type.

DESCRIPTION

Battle helmets were invariably composed of three main components, namely the helmet bowl itself and two cheek pieces, hinged to either side of the bowl. Under the Early and High Principate, the helmet consisted of a ferrous core overlain by a decorated cover or sheathing of either copper alloy (often partially tinned) or silver. Where cheek pieces were not used, there were visors on pseudo-Corinthian (and some pseudo-Attic), as well as Pfrondorf, helmets that were hinged in the same way as face-mask helmets.

Sports (face-mask) helmets were typically composed of two elements, the bowl and the face mask, which were normally hinged together. Both bowl and mask were made from wrought ferrous or copper-alloy sheet.

VARIANTS

The Early Principate

The link between the hybrid Weisenau/Imperial-Gallic helmet and the first true cavalry helmet may lie with helmets that used patterned organic materials to cover the exterior of a ferrous bowl. A find from the Kops Plateau, next to the legionary fortress on the Hunerberg at Nijmegen (Netherlands), included cavalry helmets with organic remains on the bowl (Willems 1994). Analysis showed that human, bear and horse hair were used to embroider elaborate covers for the helmet bowls (Mitschke 2007). A discovery made during gravel extraction near the legionary fortress at Xanten (Germany) had a similar covering (Kempkens in Schalles & Schreiter 1993: 113–20). These covers should not be confused with covers or bags used to protect helmets (Bishop 2025: 55) and seem to have been added as a decorative component.

Cavalry battle helmet from Witcham Gravel. (Photo © M.C. Bishop)

Related to the helmets with organic coverings may be a unique (so far) helmet found at Witcham Gravel, near Ely (England), suggested as having been deposited during the Boudican revolt of *c*.AD 60–61 (Kaminski & Sim 2014: 80). This, sometimes known as the 'bicycle bell' helmet, survives mainly as the copper-alloy sheathing, with the ferrous core almost completely corroded away. The bowl is smooth and unadorned other than tinning of its surface, but the diadem or fronton and the neck guard were decorated with large, embossed hemispheres attached with a single central rivet – hence the resemblance to an old-fashioned bicycle bell. Smaller bosses originally decorated the cheek pieces. It is possible that this helmet was originally intended to have an organic cap like the Nijmegen examples.

A find excavated from a tumulus near Weyler has become the type find for the 'Weiler' form of cavalry helmet (Fairon & Moreau-Maréchal 1983). The helmet dates from the Early Principate, the accompanying ceramic evidence suggesting that it belonged in the first half of the 1st century AD. Only the ferrous core of the helmet survived, for the most part, the bowl being worked into stylized locks of hair. The surviving ferrous cheek piece covered the ear and an embossed copper-alloy brow band ran around the front of the bowl above the rim. Tie rings were placed inside each cheek piece near the bottom and under the centre of the small neck guard. Although the cheek piece was covered with a copper-alloy skin, no traces of any such sheathing were found on the corroded bowl other than the embossed brow band. Interestingly, an unfinished copper-alloy cheek piece sheathing from the vexillation fortress at Kingsholm in Gloucester (England)

The Weyler-type battle helmet from Xanten. (Photo © M.C. Bishop)

The Xanten helmet

Discovered during archaeological work prior to quarrying for gravel in the valley of the Rhine, near the supposed location of the lost, secondary legionary fortress of Vetera near Xanten (Germany), this is a superb example of a Weyler-type cavalry battle helmet from the Early Principate. It is composed of the near-intact bowl and both cheek pieces, all three major components consisting of a ferrous core with a silver (or copper-alloy) decorated skin. Excluding cheek pieces, it measures 193mm high, 263mm front to back and 257mm in total width (Schalles & Schreiter 1993: 191).

The silver bowl skin was principally decorated with rows of stylized, raised locks of hair, around which a fire-gilded wreath of laurel leaves ran to meet at the front, on either side of a *phalera* bearing a portrait bust in high relief, possibly intended to represent a member of the imperial family. This is surrounded by depictions of weaponry, in a typical *congeries armorum* motif. The small neck guard is embossed with tendrils and cupids hunting a boar and stag. The cheek pieces include the customary moulded representation of the wearer's ears, but most of the decorated field is taken up with stylized whiskers, intended to depict sideburns or a beard. Separate ear guards have been riveted onto the bowl, as has a beaded brow band running between them.

The bowl is slightly distorted in shape and it has been suggested this may reflect an injury received by the wearer that necessitated its adaptation to match this (Prittwitz und Gaffron in Schalles & Schreiter 1993: 63). On the basis of the decoration, the date of the helmet has been suggested as the AD 40s.

The Hallaton battle helmet. (The Portable Antiquities Scheme/The Trustees of the British Museum/Wikimedia/ CC BY-SA 4.0)

did not incorporate a human ear design and its outline resembled that of an infantry helmet, possibly indicating that this was intended for a very early Weyler-type helmet.

Another possible ferrous bowl with moulded hair was recovered from the vexillation fortress at Longthorpe (England) and that dated to the middle of the 1st century AD (Frere & St Joseph 1974: 74 & Fig. 40,2). It is possible that the early Weyler-type helmets used tinning to adorn the bowl, traces of which could easily have been lost due to corrosion before, during, or after deposition.

Fragments of an undated helmet bowl from Koblenz-Bubenheim (Germany) have been identified as a sub-type of the Weyler form. A copper-alloy sheathing, again with embossed curls of hair, over an iron core now incorporated a fronton (Negin 2015).

Another battle helmet with a fronton came from a pit on a native British ritual site at Hallaton (England). This consisted of a ferrous core with gilded silver sheathing and was found with six (and a fragment of a seventh) matching cheek pieces of varying designs (Score 2011: 61–66; Sharp 2021). With its physical form painstakingly reconstructed from many fragments, the task then began of interpreting the heavily corroded details worked into the silver sheathing. With careful deduction, along with some guesswork, two possible versions were ultimately produced, although it was unclear whether the curls of hair depicted on other helmets were also used here (Sharp 2024: 41). This unique find has been dated to the early years of the Roman invasion of Britain. Whether the Hallaton helmet was a diplomatic gift, booty or the possession of a Briton serving with the Romans is unclear.

By the Flavian period, the ferrous core of such helmets was no longer embossed, as an example from a pit at Newstead (Scotland) demonstrated (Curle 1911: 164), relying instead on an embossed decorative sheathing over that core. One of the most complete examples of such a helmet, recovered during dredging operations near Xanten, featured gilded silver sheathing over its ferrous core (Schalles & Schreiter 1993: 59–63). It retains the small neck guard seen on other Weyler-type helmets, as well as the cheek pieces fully covering the ears of the wearer. The embossed, decorated brow band is still present and, as with the Hallaton helmet, the bowl is encircled by an embossed laurel wreath and there is a portrait bust (probably a member of the imperial family) in the centre of the brow region.

B **TYPES OF EARLY PRINCIPATE CAVALRY HELMET**

As cavalry changed under the Early Principate, so did their equipment, particularly their helmets. First, infantry helmets seem to have been modified to meet the unique requirements of mounted troops, particularly the incorporation of a face mask, probably for training purposes (**1**). This soon evolved into using a ferrous core with an overlying decorative skin of a non-ferrous metal such as copper alloy or even silver (**2**). In some cases, the face mask was retained, when needed, before the battle helmets and 'sports' helmet forms diverged. The earliest true cavalry battle helmets were the Weyler type, named after an example from a tumulus in Belgium (**3**). This form is shown on tombstones and represented by examples from Xanten (**4**) in Germany and Hallaton (**5**) in England.

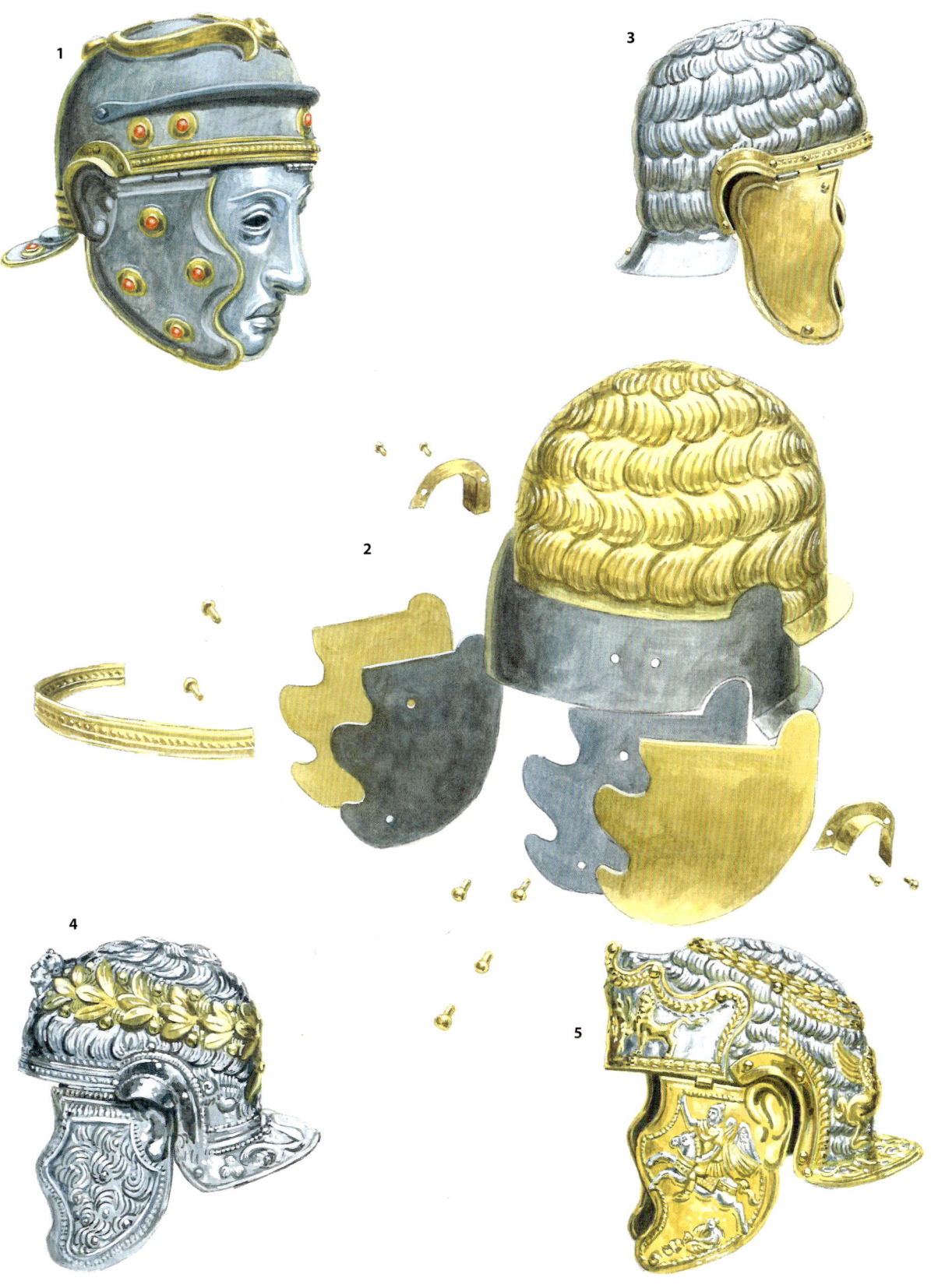

The pseudo-Attic helmet from Guisborough. (Photo © Trustees of the British Museum)

The High Principate

A helmet casing of brass from Guisborough (England) typifies the pseudo-Attic form of helmet (Sim & Kaminski 2017). Its form incorporated a decorated, embossed visor-like fronton. Adorned with embossed and incised designs, it was originally gilded and only around 0.4mm in thickness. A series of rivet holes suggest its means of attachment to its missing core. This helmet casing is matched by examples found at Chalon-sur-Saône (France) and Războieni-Cetate (Romania). A pseudo-Attic helmet bowl casing has also been found in the Wentsum River at Worthing in Norfolk (England), while a visor that almost certainly belonged with it, was found at the same location.

One of the most elaborate variants of this type was found on the site of the *cohors equitata* fort at Theilenhofen (Germany) on the Upper German and Raetian frontier of the empire. The *cohors III Bracaraugustanorum equitata* was based there and originated in what is modern-day Portugal. An infantry helmet of theirs is also known from the site (Bishop 2025: 25). The cavalry battle helmet, which bears an inscription naming the unit, has

TYPES OF HIGH PRINCIPATE CAVALRY HELMET
The 2nd century AD witnessed a new form of cavalry helmet emerging. It still has a small neck guard and copper-alloy sheathing over an iron core (**1**). Examples of the pseudo-Attic helmet type are known from Guisborough (**2**) in England and Chalon-sur-Saône (**3**) in France, while a more elaborate version, including and eagle crest, was found at Theilenhofen (**4**) in Germany. A variant of this featuring an extended crest in the form of a stretched aquiline peak is seen from Ostrov (**5**) in Romania, as well as an unprovenanced example from the former Guttmann collection, both of which featured an aventail of scale armour instead of an integral rigid neck guard.

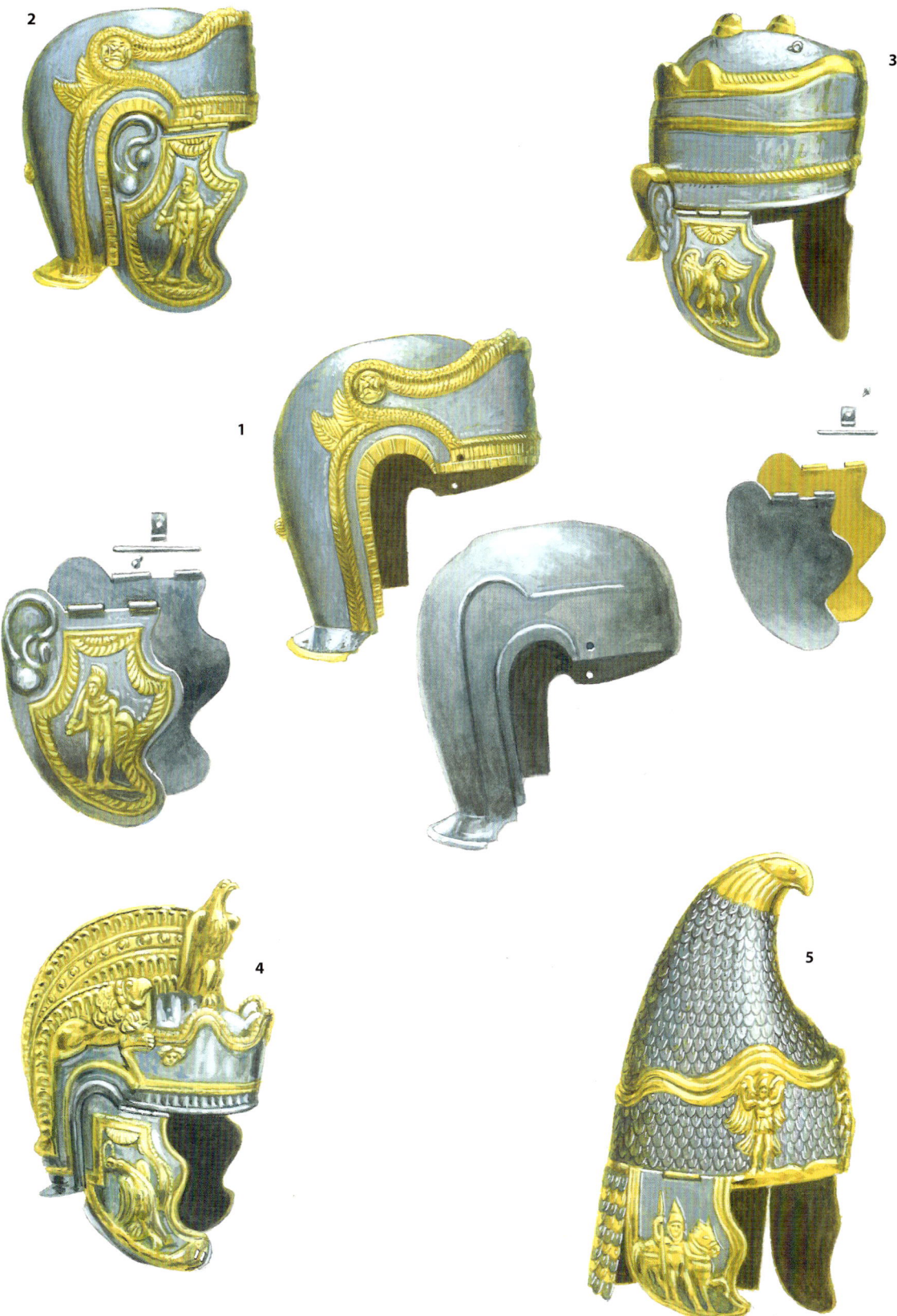

the same basic pseudo-Attic form but incorporates an eagle in a stylized crest. Although often (inaccurately) described as a 'parade' or 'officer's' helmet, other inscriptions show it variously to have been the property of two ordinary troopers (see p.58). It is richly decorated with raised detail on all of its surfaces, each cheek piece adorned with an eagle clutching a wreath, highlighted with selective tinning.

Some of the more extreme variants on the basic pseudo-Attic form display a modified bowl, raised to an eagle's head and neck in the case of an unprovenanced example in a private collection (which also replaces the neck guard with an aventail of scales) and a similar helmet from Ostrov (Romania).

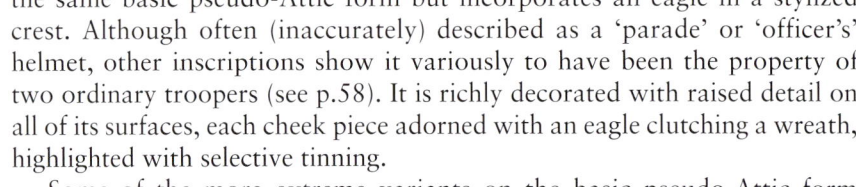

The Late Principate

The archetypal pseudo-Corinthian helmet was found in the fort at Frankfurt-Heddernheim (Lindenschmit 1900: Band 4 Taf.20). The type is so named because of its resemblance to a classical Greek Corinthian helmet pushed back onto the top of the head when not actually in combat, even down to vestigial facial features on the front of the bowl, on what is effectively a peak or brow guard. The evolved form was made of copper alloy and was thus a departure from the ferrous core and copper-alloy casing of earlier types. It featured a fixed crest with an eagle terminal at the front, but the most significant difference from earlier cavalry helmets was the replacement of the usual cheek pieces with a one-piece visor hinged to the bowl at the front, and furnished with a T-shaped opening corresponding to the area of the eyes and mouth of the wearer. This was the next logical step from large cheek pieces that overlapped and were fastened centrally, as seen on contemporary infantry helmets (Bishop 2025: 52). The visor was secured by means of studs on either side of it joined by a strap passing around the base of the neck at the back. As with the preceding types of cavalry helmet, the pseudo-Corinthian type retained a small neck guard without a carrying handle, distinguishing it from contemporary infantry headgear (Bishop 2025: 54).

While the Heddernheim example is the most complete so far found, examples of similar bowls come from Szőny (the legionary fortress of Brigetio in Hungary) and Rusovce (Gerulata in Slovakia). Similar visors are known from Rodez (France) and Ascheberg (Germany).

The Worthing visor was found in the same location (but not at the same time) as the pseudo-Attic cavalry helmet bowl (see p.24), which begs the question of whether these two disparate elements belonged together. The visor originally had a hinge in the centre front and the pseudo-Attic bowl has a rivet at the front that secures a rectangular plate on the inside, which was broken off on its lower edge and probably represents a hinge plate (Toynbee & Clarke 1948: 20), so there are good reasons to suspect that they belong together. If Fischer is correct about the attribution of pseudo-Attic and pseudo-Corinthian helmets to the 2nd and 3rd centuries AD respectively, then this looks like

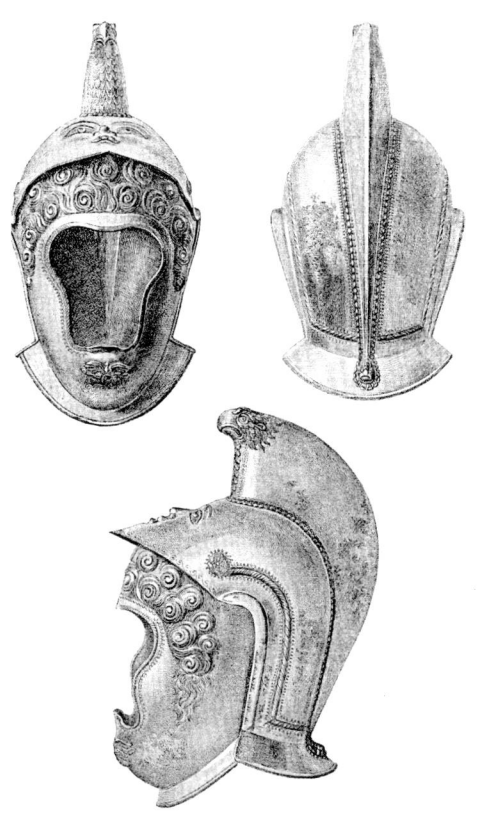

Pseudo-Corinthian battle helmet from Heddernheim. (Lindenschmit/Public Domain)

a hybrid form, not least because the helmet bowl does not have any rivet holes for cheek pieces as might be expected with a standard pseudo-Attic helmet. The Worthing visor lacks any means of attaching a T-shaped face mask so it more closely conforms to pseudo-Corinthian types rather than the Pfrondorf helmet.

Another type of helmet probably belongs with this group of Late Principate battle helmets. First found as a bowl with a high eagle *protome* protruding forward from the bowl at Vechten (Netherlands), its shape suggested that it belonged with a face mask (one was subsequently found nearby). Another example came from Islaz (Romania; Rațiu *et al.* 2023). Such a visor may also be represented by a find from the bog deposit at Thorsberg Moor (Germany; Matešić 2016). Either way, the small neck guard and absence of a carrying handle ensure the identification of this type as a cavalry helmet. The Vechten bowl and visor suggest a development from the peak of the pseudo-Corinthian, leading to the raised peak of the visor and reduced frontal area of the bowl. The Islaz helmet holds one final surprise: the bowl was formed from two halves, riveted and soldered together (Rațiu *et al.* 2023: 675). Whether the junction between the two halves was overlain by a strip, similar to that found on later ridge helmets, is unknown.

The next (and final) development in cavalry battle helmets of the Principate would see them rejoin the developmental arc of face-mask helmets, which up to this point had retained their own functional (and to some extent decorative) niche, separate from combat equipment (see p.50).

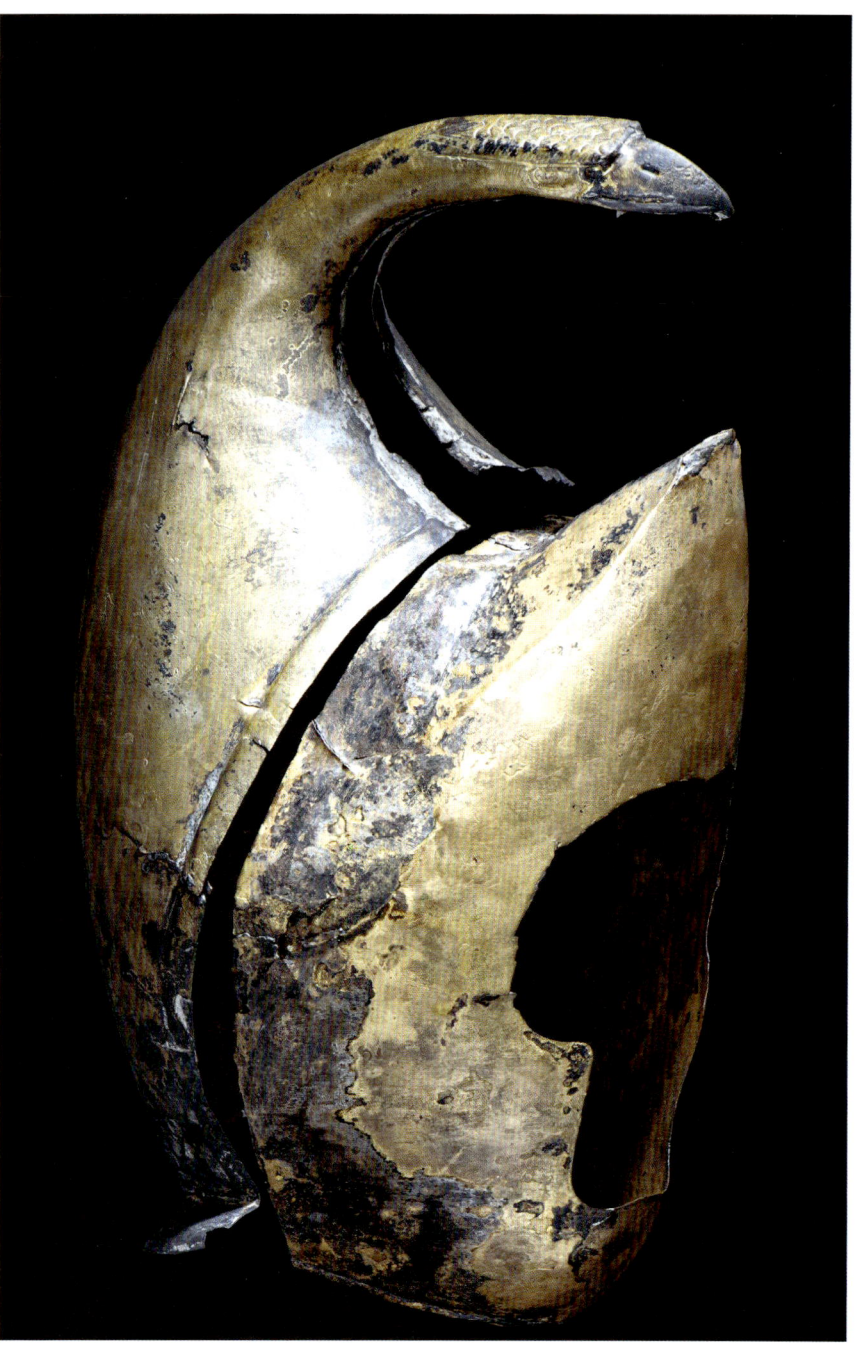

Variant of the pseudo-Corinthian battle helmet from Vechten with a pronounced eagle *protome*. (National Museum of Antiquities, Leiden/CC0 1.0)

D **TYPES OF LATE PRINCIPATE CAVALRY HELMET**

Cheek pieces of Late Principate infantry helmets had grown ever larger, to the point where they overlapped in the front and effectively formed a visor. A pseudo-Attic helmet from the Wentsum River at Worthing in Norfolk (England) came from the same location as a one-piece visor and the two had clearly originally been paired (**1**). The helmet bowl was not equipped with cheek pieces but rather had the remains of a central hinge to attach the visor. This therefore appears to be an adaptation of the pseudo-Attic type bringing it closer to the pseudo-Corinthian helmet type, typified by the finds from Heddernheim (**2**, **3**) in Germany and Vechten (**4**) in the Netherlands. A final stage of development seems to be represented by the Pfrondorf helmet (**5**) from Germany, the helmet bowl and visor of which had a detachable mask added, thereby once again unifying cavalry battle and face-mask helmets, removing the need for some cavalrymen to own two helmets (one for battle and another for training and display).

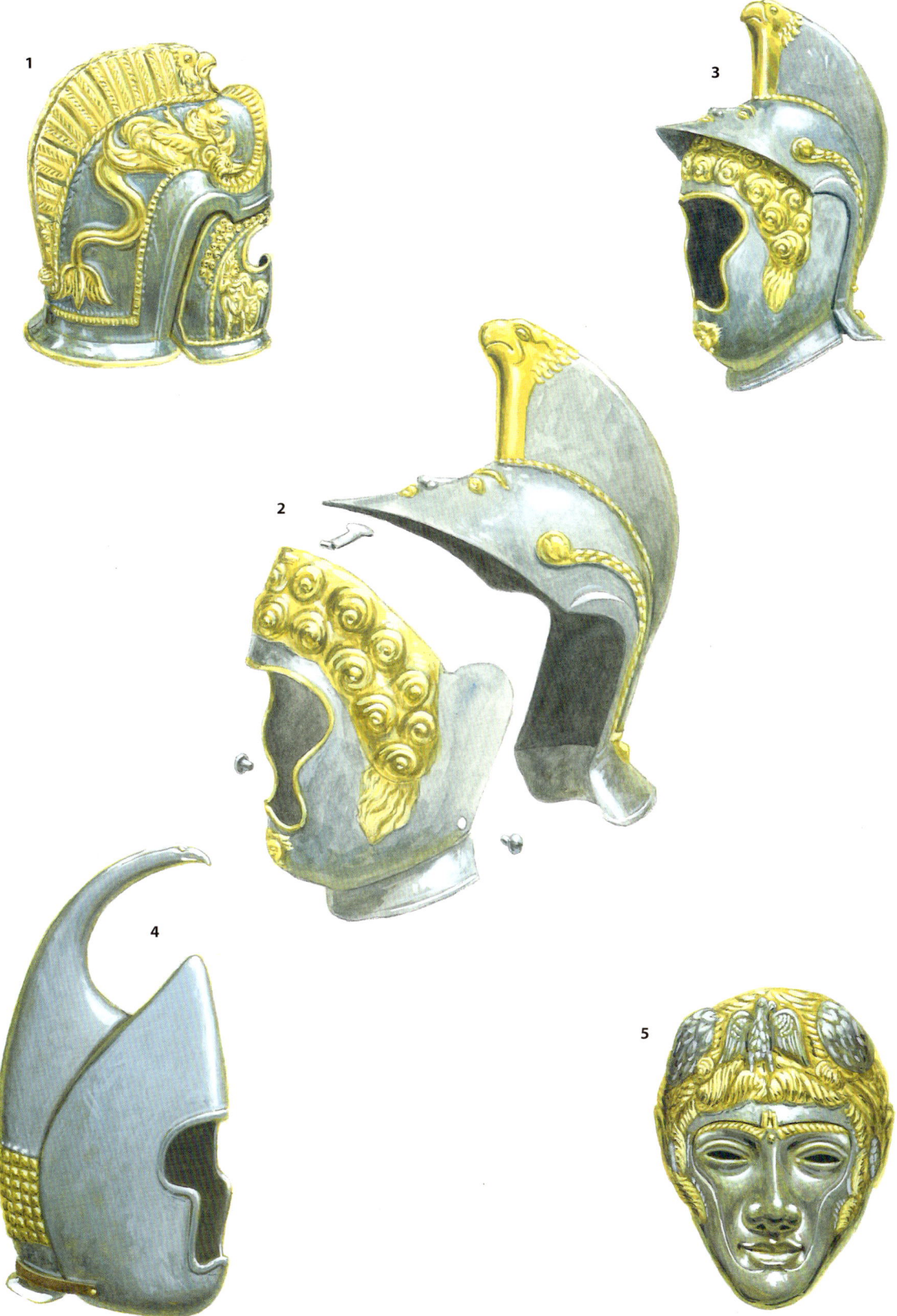

Face-mask helmets

A face mask found in a burial at Chassenard (France) is one of the earliest full-face masks that incorporated representations of the ears it covered. This was recovered along with other military equipment and coins of Gaius (Caligula, r. AD 37–41) and suggests a date towards the end of the first half of the 1st century AD. Significantly, the shape of the mask now required a matching bowl that differed markedly from cavalry battle-helmets.

Another burial, this time in Hellange (Luxembourg), also contained a face mask, but of copper alloy. A copper-alloy face-mask from the Fossa Drusiana (Netherlands) is arguably also an early example of a front element of a two-part face-mask 'sports' helmet.

Components of several face-mask helmets were recovered from pits dating from the latter part of the second half of the 1st century AD (or even early 2nd century AD) outside the fort at Newstead, as well as other items associated with the *hippika gymnasia* (ritual 'horse exercise' tournaments performed by cavalry units), such as leather chamfrons and an eye guard from horse armour. These retain the same androgynous features found on the earliest masks, but development of the embossed adornment of the helmet bowls had proceeded apace. Perhaps the most famous example of this type of face-mask helmet is that recovered from a hoard of material in a chest, probably originally buried in the corner of the fort at Ribchester (England) and now in the British Museum (Kaminski & Sim 2019).

Comparatively few face-mask helmets can confidently be ascribed to the High Principate, although some at least of those found in the Late Principate may date back to that period. The face-mask helmet found at Nawa, however, together with a combat helmet (see p.30), seems to belong in this category. Like its companion, the helmet was decorated with embossed figures in a similar style (Abdul-Hak 1954–55: 167–68). Unusually, the face featured a moustache, suggesting a measure of personalization and perhaps even a portrait of its owner.

Face-mask helmets found in the Late Principate (but probably originating in the High Principate) had largely shed the androgynous appearance of

LEFT
Face mask from the burial at Chassenard. (Cangaboda/Wikimedia/CC BY-SA 4.0)

RIGHT
Kops Plateau face mask and textile-covered helmet bowl. (Valkhof Museum/CC0)

The Crosby Garrett helmet

Found by metal detectorists in 2010 (Breeze & Bishop 2013) near the village of Crosby Garrett, this brass face-mask helmet provided a missing link in the themed examples from the Later Principate. Although Greek and Amazon masks (*personae*) were known from a number of finds, this was the first Trojan example to be recognized. Inevitably, soon after it was discovered, it was realized that a second, less complete example was already known, albeit mistakenly identified as being a Parthian helmet (James 2014). The helmet, as reconstructed, is 407mm high, 225mm wide and 263mm from front to back.

The mask (which was found almost intact) portrays the face of a young man, but retains the androgynous quality seen in earlier face masks, lacking the masculine lines of the Greeks masks or the feminine softness of the Amazon masks. The area of the skin has been selectively tinned, while three rows of luxuriant locks of hair have been left natural brass. The mouth is slightly open, as are the nostrils and the eyes, each of which has iris rings characteristic of late 2nd-/early 3rd-century AD cavalry sports masks.

The bowl (which was crushed when discovered) imitates a Phrygian cap, a type of headgear which, for the Romans, was synonymous with Asia Minor. On the Dura-Europos shield paintings (Breeze & Bishop 2013: 42–43), Trojans are habitually depicted wearing caps, while Greeks wear helmets. There is a very small neck guard and, above that, a single row of curls below a raised, upward curling ridge, to which rings were attached (presumably intended for horsehair streamers and to secure the rear of a crest box). The apex of the bowl bears a cast figuring of a griffin, which probably served to secure the front of the crest by means of a ring at the front. Below the griffin is an oval setting, which may once have held a blue glass-paste jewel similar to those on the foreheads of Amazon face masks: another stereotype for Easterners.

The mask was attached to the bowl at the top and front by means of a concealed internal hinge, and secured to the wearer by means of a stud on either side of the mask, which will have carried a simple leather strap around the base of the helmet bowl.

Trojan face-mask helmet from Crosby Garrett. (Photo © M.C. Bishop)

earlier examples and were themed with character types from the Trojan War. The three principal types were a male Greek (resembling known portraiture of Alexander the Great), a female form assumed to represent Amazons and one wearing a Phrygian cap, which probably depicted Trojans.

A notable hoard of face-mask helmets (and other 'sports' armour) of both Greek and Amazon types was found at a villa near the fort of Straubing–Sorviodurum (Germany) and probably belonged to the unit based there, the *cohors I Flavia Canathenorum milliaria sagittariorum*, a mixed unit of infantry and horse archers (Keim & Klumbach 1976). This collection of seven face masks and one associated bowl included two of the three types associated with the Trojan War, namely four Greeks (male) and three Amazons (female). The masculine features of the Greek type contrast somewhat with the earlier androgynous face masks, the hair in each case more than a little reminiscent of portraits of Alexander the Great (who was, of course, Macedonian, but to Romans this may not have mattered). The Amazons possessed feminine features and elaborately piled coiffure similar to the wigs popular with Roman women and small, blue glass-paste jewels on the forehead. A third

Face mask from the helmet recovered from the Fossa Drusiana near Leiden. (National Museum of Antiquities, Leiden/ CC0 1.0)

category of helmet was found at Crosby Garrett (England), stereotyped as a Trojan by means of its depiction of a Phrygian cap and, like the Amazons, a setting for a glass-paste jewel at the base of a griffon-shaped crest-holder (Breeze & Bishop 2013: 7–13, Fig.10). Another bowl of the Trojan type has been identified in the collection of the Boston Museum of Fine Arts (James 2014).

Arrian makes no mention of themed teams in his description of the *hippika gymnasia*, stating only that *turma* (squadron) competed against *turma* (and only two at a time). Thus, these distinct 'characters' suggest

E

FACE-MASK CAVALRY HELMETS

Face-mask (or 'sports') helmets were highly specialized pieces of equipment, only used by the best troopers in each *turma* during the exercises described by Arrian and termed by him the *hippika gymnasia*. Construction was simple, with just a face mask hinged to a bowl, the whole assembly being secured by a leather strap passing from either side of the mask around the back of the bowl (**1**). The first independent form of face-mask helmet is represented by finds with a mask attached to a plain ferrous bowl covered with woven textile (**2**). Helmets became ever more elaborately decorated, culminating in examples like the Ribchester (England) helmet towards the end of the Early Principate (**3**). By the latter part of the High and into the Late Principate, face-mask helmets were themed around the Trojan War. There were Greeks, represented here by a helmet from Herzogenburg (**4**) in Austria (possibly originally from the nearby fort at Traismauer); Amazons, like an example from Eining (**5**) in Germany; while a Trojan helmet can be seen in **Plate H**.

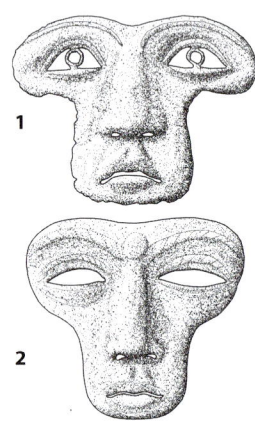

T-shaped face masks of Pfrondorf-type helmets, from (**1**) Mainz and (**2**) Weißenburg. (Drawing © M.C. Bishop)

that the exercise had subtly evolved during the 2nd century AD, possibly due to a persistent interest in the subject of the Trojan War, seen elsewhere in the *lusus Troiae* ('Trojan games') revived by Augustus (and described by Vergil, *Aeneid* 5.545–603) and later on the decoration of the oval shields from Dura-Europos (Syria), where the same stereotypes can be seen (Breeze & Bishop 2013: 42–43).

Face-mask helmets were reunited with battle helmets with the adoption of the Pfrondorf type. Taking the bowl and visor concept first seen with the pseudo-Corinthian type to its next logical step, provision was made to add a face mask within the T-shaped aperture in the visor. Besides the near-complete example from Pfrondorf itself, a bowl and visor of this type (albeit possibly not a matching pair) are known from Ostrov, while T-shaped face masks come from a number of sites, including Mainz, Weißenburg (both Germany) and Sotin (Croatia). The obvious advantage of the design was that a cavalryman no longer needed two helmets, one for battle and one for the *hippika gymnasia*, and would thus cost him less. As Lindenschmit noted (1881: Heft 5 Taf.4), inserting and removing the face mask would not have been instantaneous, because it was attached by means of a turning pin at the top and a tongue-and-slot system at the bottom. Nevertheless, it *was* removable. This ingenious device also serves to confirm that obscured vision was considered undesirable in combat (see p.53).

Thus a dual-function helmet was produced and this probably coincided with the last stages of the *hippika gymnasia* in the Roman auxiliary cavalry. Masked 'sports' helmets were no longer to be made under the Dominate, but by this time the heavy cavalry of the Sassanian *clibanarii* were evidently using face masks:

> However, all were covered over every limb with close-fitting plates in such a way that the rigid junctions matched the joints of the limbs, and likenesses of human faces were so carefully fitted to their heads that, on their solid, armoured bodies, missiles could lodge only where small openings placed over the eyes limited sight, or through the upper parts of the nostrils, where a narrow breath of air was exhaled. (Ammianus Marcellinus 25.1.12, tr. author)

As elaborate manoeuvres were not required of them, situational awareness was less likely to be a concern. It might be argued that Ammianus' interest in this could well be taken to indicate that this practice was not common among the Roman heavy cavalry of his day.

Greek helmet face-masks from Straubing. (Carole Raddato/ Wikimedia/CC BY-SA 2.0)

DOMINATE CAVALRY HELMETS

As was the case with infantry helmets, those of the cavalry underwent yet another significant transformation from earlier designs under the Dominate. The intricate shapes characteristic of the Principate were largely replaced by simpler, composite constructions that were far easier to produce. The exception was the retention of enhancing a ferrous core with a decorative sheathing in a different metal, usually gilded silver. As far as can be determined, this shift aligned with a broader change in the production of military equipment, which came to be organized through a network of state-run *fabricae* (see p.42). Once again, external influences appear to have played a role, as evidenced by a Sassanid Persian helmet discovered in a mid-3rd-century AD siege mine at Dura-Europos, foreshadowing the developments seen in Dominate-era helmets (James 1986).

HISTORY

There seems to be a 'missing link' between that helmet excavated at Dura-Europos and the first ridge helmets, which were the predominant form of head protection under the Dominate. A hint at what we might be missing is perhaps provided by the bipartite Islaz helmet bowl (see p.27), but it is always salutary to remember how many helmets must have been in use at any one time compared with how many have actually survived (and been recovered). All that is known is that by the end of the 3rd century AD, helmet bowls were essentially produced in two halves, one to either side, joined by a strip or ridge running from front to back. Both infantry and cavalry helmets had separate cheek pieces and neck guards, distinguished mainly by the form of the cheek pieces and brow band for the two different troop types.

Dura Sasanian helmet. (Yale University Art Gallery Dura-Europos Collection)

Key to confirming the identification of cavalry helmets of the Dominate is the example from Peel near Deurne (Netherlands). The Peel helmet is one of a group, usually identified as Berkasovo-type helmets, that are named after two examples from that site in what is now Serbia. Found in a bog together with a number of other items (Braat *et al.* in Klumbach 1973: 52–56; Dolmans 2018), most of the ferrous core did not survive, but the decorative gilded silver outer sheathing preserved the form of the helmet. The fact that it bore an inscription (STABLESIA VI) naming the unit to which it had belonged – the *vexillatio comitatensis stablesiani VI* – enables it to be identified as a cavalry helmet. Units of *stablesiani* are attested around the empire in the *Notitia Dignitatum*.

The final development was another external import and only seems to have become significant after the fall of the Western Empire: the arrival of *Spangenhelme* (literally 'braced helmets') from the steppe regions to the east. Made up of separate plates, these were popular with the barbarian peoples Rome encountered to the east (they are even depicted on

Trajan's Column), but probably only really adopted by the Byzantine Army. An undated example from Dayr al-Madīnah (Egypt) follows the general form of the ridge-type cavalry helmets in terms of its large cheek pieces and nasal, but has its neck guard attached by rivets and the cheek pieces hinged to the bowl.

DESCRIPTION

Cavalry helmets under the Dominate, as has just been mentioned, were constructed from a series OF distinct components, namely the multipartite bowl (including a brow band and nasal or nose guard), the cheek pieces and the neck guard.

As with infantry helmets, the two halves of the bowl were riveted together by means of a central raised bar. There was a series of holes around the bowl rim and these served for stitching a leather liner to the interior. Miks (2014: 30–32 & Abb.24) has identified two principal bowl variants, each with two sub-types. The first variant either has a six-part (hexapartite) bowl, with a broad band running side to side (e.g. Peel), or a four-part (quadripartite) bowl with the quadrants joined by a narrow bowl from side to side (e.g. Berkasovo 1). The second variant has a two-part (bipartite) bowl, either with (e.g. Koblenz) or without (e.g. Budapest) small ear openings in the bowl rim and cheek pieces. Additionally, a brow band could incorporate a nasal. Cheek pieces were not hinged to the bowl but rather attached by means of leather straps, either fastened with buckles through slots in the respective components, or riveted to them. The cheek pieces of cavalry helmets covered the ear, unlike infantry ridge helmets, although some incorporated pierced ear covers. Presumably, as in earlier periods, this was because vocal commands were not important for Roman cavalry units, unlike visual instructions with the standards or audible commands from musical instruments. Ridge helmets were also equipped with a separate neck guard, similarly attached to the bowl using straps, once more utilizing buckled or riveted straps.

Echoing earlier cavalry helmet construction, the ferrous core of each major component was covered by gilded silver sheathing. This sheathing could be decorated with embossing and, in some instances, with fake jewels within settings in a variety of shapes.

The Dayr al-Madīnah helmet, like all *Spangenhelme*, featured a rim with a framework of bands with plates between them forming a more conical bowl shape than was the case with ridge helmets.

The Dayr al-Madīnah *Spangenhelm* from Egypt. (Author's collection, Public Domain)

VARIANTS

The Peel or Deurne helmet (see p.38), arguably one of the best-known ridge helmets, has undergone intensive study prior to the production of a replica (Dolmans 2018). While it is unique, it is nevertheless comparable to Berkasovo 1, Budapest and Concești (Klumbach 1973: 9).

Two helmets are known from near Berkasovo, not far from what was the Roman city of Sirmium, and were found together with a snaffle bit and propeller-shaped belt fittings (Manojlović-Marijanski in Klumbach 1973: 15–38). Berkasovo 1 features a prominent raised fore-and-aft ridge, supported on rivets. The decorative panels divide the bowl into four, two on either side, and these are elaborately embellished with round, oval, rectangular and lozenge-shaped glass-paste jewel settings. Similar settings are to be found on the cheek pieces and the neck guard. A brow band, slightly arched over the eyes, is held in place with spherical-headed rivets and terminates in a central nasal. The helmet bears an inscription in Greek: 'Dizzon, use with good health. Product of Avitus' (see p.58). Berkasovo 2 more closely resembles the Peel helmet (hence they are often referred to as of the Berkasovo type). Berkasovo 2 only has two panels on the bowl, one either side of the raised central ridge, and its decoration is more restrained than either its companion piece or the Peel example. There are the customary cheek pieces, neck guard (with a pair of buckles) and a brow band with nasal. This too bears an inscription, this time in Latin and less certain.

The Budapest helmet was found on the Pest (Hungary) side of the Danube River near the southern corner tower of the Diocletianic fort (often referred to as Contra Aquincum) on the opposite riverbank to the legionary fortress

The Peel (Deurne) helmet

The Peel helmet, found near Deurne in the Netherlands, is a near-complete outer sheathing, although its ferrous core had largely decayed *in situ*, which means its original dimensions are uncertain. The helmet was probably originally 177mm high, 180–90mm wide and 210–20mm long, however (Dolmans 2018: 229). It was found along with other items, including a crossbow brooch, a bell, a spur, a shoe, the components of a leather tent and textile fragments (Braat in Klumbach 1973: 51–84). A *terminus post quem* ('limit after which') is provided by coins of Constantine the Great (r. AD 306–37), the latest (unworn) coin dating to AD 319. The assemblage appears incomplete, however, and may not have been recovered in its entirety.

Detailed study of the helmet has revealed that some errors were made in the early conservation attempts (Dolmans 2018: 229–30) because, in common with most Roman helmets recovered from the archaeological record, it is not 'as found' and has undergone some reconstruction. The bowl is composed of six decorative gilded silver panels, three on either side of the central ridge, each with decorative borders and centrally embossed with an anchor motif, adopted into Christian symbology by the 4th century AD (Hoss & Verstegen 2025: 136). The neck guard was attached to the bowl by means of a pair of buckles, as was probably the case with the cheek pieces (Dolmans 2018: 230). A brow band, arched over each eye, descends in the centre to form a nasal. There is no obvious means to attach a crest to the apex of the bowl.

The helmet bears an incised inscription on the side of the bowl naming the cavalry unit to which it belonged (see p.35) and on the neck guard 'M. Titus Lunamis 1 pound 1½ ounces', presumed to be the name of the *barbaricarius* who decorated the helmet and the weight of the gilded silver required. Reconstructions of the helmet have a total weight of around 3.3kg each, of which 2.5kg represents the ferrous core, 368g for the gilded silver (the amount cited in the inscription), 180g for bitumen (used with tar and tallow to affix the gilded silver sheathing to the underlying ferrous plates) and about 250g for leather components like the lining, straps and ties (Dolmans 2018: 242).

of Aquincum (Thomas in Klumbach 1973: 39–50). Only parts of the bowl and cheek pieces remain, but these were all decorated with glass-paste jewel settings as with Berkasovo 1, the ferrous core being heavily corroded but still present. The bowl is in two parts divided by the central ridge and a brow band survives, but lacking its nasal.

A ridge helmet from Conceşti (Romania) was found in a grave, but has no brow band or neck guard (Skalon in Klumbach 1973: 91–94). The sheathing of the bowl consists of six components: the fore-and-aft ridge, a transverse cross-piece and four triangular plates in the spaces created within this cruciform arrangement. These elements are edged with pelleted decoration and attached by means of spherical-headed rivets. An unprovenanced helmet in a private collection bears more than a passing resemblance to the Conceşti example in terms of its form and decoration, but includes a neck guard and nasal, as well as the bowl and cheek pieces.

Jarak (Serbia), like Berkasovo, is not far from Sirmium, and has produced the decorative components of another ridge helmet (Dautova-Ruševljan & Vujović 2011). It was discovered inside a pottery vessel and was probably concealed because of the value of its decorative sheathing, which had been stripped from the ferrous core and rolled up.

Only the neck guard and cheek pieces of the San Giorgio Di Nogaro (Italy) helmet survive, but with the ferrous core mostly intact beneath the gilded silver sheathing. Enough survives to show its similarity to other helmets of the Berkasovo type.

An assemblage of 129 fragments of ridge helmets from a mid-4th-century AD pit in Koblenz has been suggested as having been set aside during the process of stripping the precious-metal sheathings from them. As well as

two Intercisa-type infantry helmets, these pieces included components of ten cavalry helmets (Miks 2014).

Although a majority of the recovered cavalry ridge helmets survive as just (apparently scavenged) decorative sheathing, there is an interesting exception. The *Notitia Dignitatum* records the garrison of the Saxon Shore fort of Gariannonum (England) as being the *Equites Stablesiani* so it is at least worth considering the helmet from Burgh Castle (England) as a Dominate cavalry helmet. Although the site has in the past been identified with this placename, it is by no means certain. Only the ferrous core of the

Ridge helmet from Jarak.
(Museum of Vojvodina/
Wikimedia/CC BY-SA 3.0 Serbia)

hexapartite bowl survives, together with a fragment of what may be a brow band and nasal. This last detail may be a more reliable indication that this was a cavalry helmet than the possible association with the unit mentioned in the *Notitia Dignitatum*.

A final category of cavalry helmet that needs to be mentioned are the *Spangenhelme* (notably of the Baldenheim type). The Dayr al-Madīnah helmet was made of ferrous material (iron or steel: no analysis has been undertaken to date) in all of its components (Dittmann 1940).

TYPES OF DOMINATE CAVALRY HELMET

Under the Dominate, multipartite ridge helmets almost completely replaced the earlier single-piece bowl types of the Principate. Bowls were constructed from two, four, or even six segments united by a ridge piece running from front to back (**1**). Cheek pieces and neck guards were attached to the bowl by means of straps and buckles. Linings were stitched to the insides of all the components. All of the cavalry helmets were distinguished from contemporary infantry helmets chiefly by their much larger, L-shaped cheek pieces. Two principal variants can be discerned, each with

sub-variants, defined by the manner in which the bowl was formed.

The helmet from Peel (Deurne) in the Netherlands represents the first variant, with a bowl made up of six plates (**2**). The second, with four plates comprising the bowl, is typified by one of the helmets from Berkasovo (**3**) in Serbia. The bejewelled Budapest helmet (**4**) from Hungary serves to demonstrate the second variant, which had a two-part bowl with no ear openings, while one of the helmets from Koblenz (**5**) in Germany was a variant on this, but with ear openings.

MANUFACTURE AND DECORATION

WORKSHOPS

It is sobering to note that even less is known about the production of Republican cavalry helmets than is the case for infantry headgear, not least because of a dearth of archaeological examples of early helmets. Vegetius intimated that Roman Army craftsmen produced helmets in the *fabricae* of legionary bases during the Principate:

> These craftsmen either produce new arms, vehicles, and all sorts of weaponry or repair those that have been damaged. They also have workshops specializing in shields, armour and bows, where they manufacture arrows, missile weapons, helmets and every type of armour. This was, in fact, their principal duty – to ensure that anything the army might need would never be lacking in the camp. (Vegetius, *DRM* 2.11, tr. author)

Nevertheless, unequivocal evidence of such production is just as difficult to identify for cavalry helmets as it is for their infantry counterparts, although indications of repair are not hard to find. An example of a ferrous face mask from the Augustan fortress of Haltern (Germany), found corroded to an anvil (Bishop & Coulston 2006: 234), is no guarantee that it was produced there, as it could merely have been undergoing repairs.

There is a tendency among modern-day scholars to attempt to identify discrete workshops when large enough quantities of material have been discovered. Cavalry helmets, whether battle or face-mask, are no exception to this. To do so, however, runs the risk of oversimplifying the means of production and distribution within the Roman Army. Attempting to identify workshops is by no means an easy task. Nevertheless, one of the Nawa helmets preserved an inscription with a craftsman's name, M. Mactorius Barbarus (*AE* 1957, 126), with the suffix FT, generally accepted as a shortening of *fecit*, indicating that he made it. The *tria nomina* (three names) indicate that he was a Roman citizen, perhaps a veteran.

State production under the Principate was undoubtedly augmented by that of civilian craftsmen, presumably veterans. Under the Dominate, however, the indications are that the production of helmets had become more centralized at specific locations around the Eastern and Western empires. It is possible they were included in the general *fabricae armorum*, as no specific helmet *fabricae* are mentioned in the *Notitia Dignitatum* (James 1988: 261).

MANUFACTURE

Vegetius' comments cited above about the manufacture of military equipment are as important for cavalry helmets as they were for those of the infantry, when discussing the craftsmen available within the Roman Army. Likewise, Justinian's *Digest*'s (50.6.7) list of *immunes* serving as specialists in the Roman Army helmet-makers (*bucularum structores*: literally 'cheek-piece makers'), quoting the 2nd-century AD jurist Tarrutienus Paternus, is just as relevant. Roman cavalry helmets, like those of the infantry, were individually produced by craftsmen, rather than being mass-produced. Components could be separately produced, using both craftsmen and semi-skilled workers, with items ultimately assembled. This would have been more efficient than the

Copper-alloy bowl (left) and mask (right) from separate 'sports' helmets from Newstead. (© M.C. Bishop & johnbod/ Wikimedia/CC BY-SA 3.0)

modern-day method employed for single-craftsman replicas, but at the same time could lead to inconsistent quality. As bronze was employed for infantry helmets in the Republican period, it is likely that the same was true for cavalry helmets. It is known that brass was used in the Late Republican/ Early Principate period and became the principal alloy of copper employed. Steel was an important constituent for cavalry helmet cores, but decorating it with raised relief (as with Early Principate helmets from Weyler and Longthorpe – see p.22) may have been more time-consuming than working with thin copper-alloy sheet overlays, and thus was abandoned.

Analysis of the Hallaton helmet (see p.22) has revealed that the gilded silver sheathing was applied to the ferrous core over a resin-like filler (Sharp 2021: 41–42), and in this it resembled the Xanten helmet (Schalles & Schreiter 1993: 59–63). This would have avoided one of the weaknesses of Roman military equipment that allowed ferrous metal and copper alloy to come into contact, namely bi-metallic corrosion, often a problem for Roman armour (Bishop 2022: 52).

Face-mask helmets were not double-skinned like cavalry battle helmets and could be wrought from either copper alloy or ferrous metal. As the examples from Newstead illustrate (see p.30), the quality of workmanship on such helmets was independent of the metal utilized. They also needed to be strong enough to resist strikes by dummy javelins.

The production of Dominate ridge helmets was simplified by producing bowls in two or more parts, as well as separate neck guards and cheek pieces. This development may, however, have been presaged by the Islaz helmet, a likely development of the Late Principate pseudo-Corinthian helmet type. While this is speculation, a more solidly founded insight into the manufacture and decoration of Dominate-era ridge helmets is provided by the *Codex Theodosianus* (a 4th–5th-century AD compilation of the laws of the Roman Empire). It preserves an interesting decree from AD 374 concerning differential rates of work between different *fabricae*:

Since at both Antioch and Constantinople, each armourer [*barbaricarius*] covers helmets [*cassides*] with bronze over a period of thirty days — six per person — and also cheek pieces [*bucculae*], and since at Antioch, eight helmets and an equal number of cheek pieces are plated with silver and gilded within thirty days, whereas at Constantinople only three helmets receive such treatment in the same period, we hereby decree that at Constantinople as well, each armourer shall decorate not eight helmets per thirty days, but six, with the same number of cheek pieces, adorned with gold and silver. (*Codex Theodosianus* 10.22.1, tr. author)

Such a *barbaricarius* appears to be named on the inscription on the neck guard of the Peel helmet (see p.38).

DECORATION

Ornament

Roman cavalry helmets, because of their high degree of decoration, and because the surviving components are perceived as being too flimsy to offer sufficient protection for use in battle, are often incorrectly described as 'parade' helmets. First, there is no evidence that the Romans had separate parade equipment that soldiers would don for parades, however they might be envisaged by a modern-day audience, in the same way that British Army Guards regiments have parade equipment for ceremonial occasions as well as camouflage fatigues for everyday use and combat (Bishop 1990: 23–25). Second, modern-day assessments of flimsiness are often only based on the copper-alloy skin, rather than both the skin and underlying ferrous core. The *hippika gymnasia* did require special equipment, but these were not parades as such, but rather training exercises with an element of display and theatre built in. Highly decorated equipment is also sometimes described as having belonged to an officer (without any overt evidence to support the claim). Indeed, helmets that might have been associated with an officer – such as the contents of the Nawa tomb – differ little from regular equipment. Thus comments about 'parade' or 'officer's' helmets in reports should always be viewed with a measure of scepticism.

Arguably, the use of copper-alloy skinning over a ferrous core enabled elaborate relief and engraved decoration to be incorporated into cavalry

RIGHT
The Ribchester face-mask helmet. (Rex Harris/Wikimedia/ CC BY 2.0)

FAR RIGHT
Face mask from the Tell 'Umm Hōrān 'sports' helmet found in the burial near Nawa. (Photo © J.C.N. Coulston)

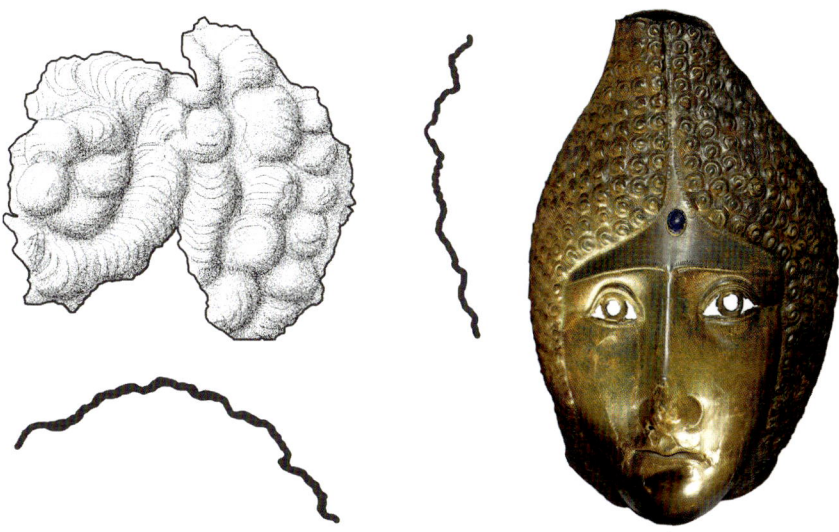

battle helmets. This is not to say that ferrous helmets could not be adorned with raised detail, as several face-mask helmets and even some battle helmets demonstrate. The depiction of locks of hair on the bowls of both principal types of helmet formed one of the most popular motifs during the Early Principate and continued with face-mask helmets into the Late Principate. Cheek pieces could be adorned with mythological motifs (Jupiter, Mars or the brothers Castor and Pollux, for example) as well as martial themes such as shields. Battle and face-mask helmets came to incorporate diadems or wreaths into the stylized hair, but there are also examples of both types with figural decoration on the bowl, such as was the case with the two helmets from Nawa (possibly depicting aspects of Lucius Verus' eastern wars) and face-mask helmets from Ribchester (a battle between infantry and cavalry) and Newstead (Cupid driving a chariot), the latter lacking its mask. The theme of the Trojan War, apparently developed in the High to Late Principate, served to unify the face-mask helmets into three broad character strands: Greek, Amazon and Trojan. The Xanten Weyler-type helmet is decorated with stylized locks of hair and a laurel wreath with a central *phalera* on the forehead featuring a raised portrait bust, possibly depicting a member of the imperial family. The cheek pieces and visors of the pseudo-Attic and -Corinthian types include similar motifs. The Worthing mask, for example, incorporated repoussé depictions of Mars and Victoria.

Inscribed floral designs can be seen on the Late Principate Crosby Garrett and Islaz helmets and both of these pieces are surprisingly understated, compared to some of the relief decoration on the (probably earlier) pseudo-Attic battle helmets.

Just as cavalry helmets under the Principate employed copper-alloy (or occasionally silver) skins over a ferrous core, Later Roman ridge helmets (both infantry and cavalry) did the same, with gilded silver over the core. Again, this seems to have been standard practice for all helmets, not just for officers' or ceremonial headgear.

By the time of the Dominate, with Christianity already present in the Roman Army even before its official adoption as the state religion by Constantine the Great, its symbology could be found decorating Roman military equipment. Classical mythological scenes were no longer favoured.

The Peel helmet bears anchors, a well-known Christian symbol, while the Chi-Rho christogram can be found adorning some helmets on the nasal, as with that from Alsóhetény (Hungary). The glass-paste jewels adorning some helmets, like the Berkasovo 1 and Budapest examples, might not have been used purely for aesthetic reasons and may have had an apotropaic function. Constantine's mother, the Empress Helena, on a mission in the Holy Land to find evidence for the site of the crucifixion of Jesus Christ for her son, collected what she believed were parts of the true cross and nails from it: 'The mother of the emperor, on learning the accomplishment of her desire, gave orders that a portion of the nails should be inserted in the royal helmet, in order that the head of her son might be preserved from the darts of his enemies' (Theodoret, *Ecclestiastical History* 1.17, tr. Schaaff).

Cresting

Roman cavalry headgear, both battle and face-mask helmets, bore crests and plumes. The Republican cavalryman depicted wearing a Boeotian (or derivative) helmet on the so-called Altar of Domitius Ahenobarbus has what appears to be a horsehair plume hanging down from the apex of the bowl. In his account of the *hippika gymnasia*, Arrian noted that in the Early Principate, 'Helmet crests made of light-coloured hair hang down from the helmets and have no practical purpose, but only serve as an ornament. They flutter when the horses trot, even if there is only a slight breeze, and they are a fine sight' (Arrian, *Tēch. Takt.* 34, tr. author).

Figural tombstones often depict cavalrymen with crests and plumes on their helmets. The Early Principate relief of Flavinus of the *ala Petriana* was depicted in profile with a fore-and-aft crest flanked by plumes on either side of his helmet. Insus, a trooper of the *ala Augusta* based in Lancaster (England), is depicted looking directly at the viewer but seems to have the same arrangement of a central crest and flanking plumes. Flavius Bassus, an *eques* of the *ala Noricorum*, on the other hand, is shown without crest or plumes on his tombstone from Köln and the same is true of several other Rhineland cavalry tombstones.

Actual examples of crest and plume fittings are also archaeologically attested, although some helmets, such as the Xanten Weyler-type example, show no signs of attachments. Plume tubes usually took the form of a cylinder riveted to the side of the helmet in the region of the temples. A plume – probably just a feather or group of feathers set into a metal base – would simply be inserted into the tube when required. Fore-and-aft crests were more complex, in that they needed a central support and attachment points (a hook to take a loop or a ring to provide a tie point) on the front and back of the helmet bowl. The Ribchester helmet has rings at the top front and rear of the bowl but no obvious means of support for a crest at the apex so these may have been intended for streamers. The Crosby Garrett helmet employed a cast copper-alloy griffin soldered to the top of the bowl to provide support for the front of a crest in a similar manner to that depicted on a statue of Mars from Rome, on which a sphinx figurine is shown used in this way. The Crosby Garrett helmet also had a row of rings across the occipital region at the back of the bowl, possibly for attaching coloured horsehair streamers.

Most helmets from the Dominate era lack any obvious means of attaching a separate crest box, although the Budapest helmet is a notable exception, with buckles surviving to either side of the apex and at the front and back of the bowl. The most logical interpretation of these is to affix a crest box.

Fore-and-aft crest (highlighted in blue) and side plumes (red) depicted on the helmet of Flavinus on his tombstone from Hexham Abbey in England. (Photo © M.C. Bishop)

MAINTENANCE

Vegetius' description of the duties of a *decurio* (the officer in charge of a *turma* of cavalry) recalls other writers' comments about the psychological effect of shiny arms and armour, but he does not mention precisely how that weaponry should be cleaned: '[He must] insist that they frequently clean and maintain their armour, including breastplates, spears and helmets [*cassides*]. For indeed, the gleam of well-maintained armour brings great terror to the enemy. Who would believe a soldier to be warlike if his weapons are spoiled by neglect, dirt and rust?' (Vegetius, *DRM* 2.14, tr. author).

Onasander was a Greek philosopher who dedicated his work *The General* to Q. Veranius, who at one point commanded the army in Britain in AD 57 prior to his early death later that year in post. He too commented on the importance of gleaming arms and armour:

> Let it be a matter of concern for the general to deploy the army in splendour by means of its arms. This is an easy task for someone who has summoned the soldiers to sharpen their swords [*xiphē*] and to polish their helmets [*korythes*] and breastplates [*thōrakes*]. For the approaching companies appear more fearsome because of the gleam of the weapons, and many terrors that strike the soul before battle are stirred up by what the eye perceives. (Onasander, *The General* 28, tr. author)

Even though cavalry helmets throughout the Roman period made use of tinning, silvering and even gilding, this seems primarily to have been for decorative effect, rather than protection from corrosion. The encyclopaedist (and former cavalry commander) Pliny the Elder suggests various ways of cleaning different metals, but it is by no means clear whether these were tried and tested methods or merely something he was copying from other writers. His methods include using vinegar and ashes to clean copper (and presumably copper alloys: *Natural History* 34.22), as well as pumice (34.26), and emery (36.22), albeit in the context of polishing marble. To prevent the corrosion of copper alloys, he advocates rubbing items with oil (34.21), although the practicalities of an army coating its equipment with (presumably olive) oil in the field make this seem a rather unlikely option.

Cavalry helmets sometimes show evidence of repairs, even though they seem to have been less likely than their infantry counterparts to suffer combat damage. With comparatively few components, the most vulnerable parts of both battle and face-mask helmets were always those employing hinges: the cheek pieces, visors, or face masks. This explains why helmet bowls are seldom found with those hinged components, and why the hinged pieces are often found by themselves. Hence repairs to hinged items are not unknown.

Items that needed repair would be put aside for later attention. If they could not be fed back into the system then they would be recycled, either stripped of components (such as the decorative sheathing on Dominate helmets) in a process of cannibalization, or their component metalwork melted down (in the case of copper alloy) or reforged. This process required a system of static bases (like those that existed from the Early Principate onwards) to work at its most efficient.

Relief from the tombstone of the cavalryman Insus of *ala Augusta* found at Lancaster, showing the central crest and side plumes on his helmet. (Photo © M.C. Bishop)

CAVALRY HELMETS IN USE

The fact that some cavalrymen under the Principate had two helmets – a battle helmet and a face-mask (or 'sports') helmet, as in the burial at Nawa – has to be seen for what it is: unusual.

> The riders themselves, if they excel in their rank or if they are distinguished by their special riding skills, wear gilded helmets made of iron or bronze, in order to attract the attention of the audience. In contrast to the helmets intended for combat, these helmets not only protect the head and cheeks, but are also precisely adapted to the rider's face on all sides, with openings for the eyes that do not obstruct the view and yet protect it. (Arrian, *Tēch. Takt.* 34, tr. author)

It was not the case in the Republican era, however, nor under the Dominate. It is clear that an arc can be detected, whereby the bifurcation in purpose begins in the Early Principate, with face masks attached to a Weisenau/Imperial-Gallic type helmet, through to the Late Principate, when cheek pieces on pseudo-Corinthian helmets evolve into a single visor, for which a small, T-shaped mask could be attached to what was now, effectively, a dual-purpose battle and 'sports' helmet.

COMBAT

The passage from Arrian quoted above makes it quite clear both that face-mask helmets were not used in combat and that they were not used by all cavalrymen. In combat, a rider would need a regular battle helmet, although these could be just as elaborately decorated as a 'sports' helmet. The emphasis on protection offered by such helmets differed considerably from those used by infantrymen and that is apparent from various features of a cavalry combat helmet.

The first thing to consider is the neck guard. These were always kept small on cavalry battle helmets, whereas infantry helmets saw them

---

G **REPUBLICAN CAVALRY HELMETS IN USE**

While the Lacus Curtius relief in Rome (see p.52) is an Early Principate copy of the original, it is generally assumed that is shows a view of what a mid-Republican cavalryman might have worn. It depicts a fully armed horseman riding into a fissure that had opened in the Forum Romanum, sacrificing himself in order to save Rome (the fissure closing after him). As it was a Republican view of what a cavalryman might have looked like in mythological times, it is reasoned that he is depicted wearing contemporary equipment. Our reconstruction (**1**) wears a short, muscled cuirass (with a double row of *pteryges* visible below the waist) and carries a circular *parma* in his left hand and a thrusting spear in his right. On his head he wears a Montefortino helmet with a red horsehair crest. His horse has a simple pad saddle and blanket.

The so-called Altar of Domitius Ahenobarbus offers us a rare glimpse of a Late Republican cavalryman in the context of a census and military levy alongside legionary infantrymen. He is shown here (**2**) wearing a mail shirt, split at the hem on either side over a tunic and barely visible arming garment. He is equipped with a circular *parma* in his left hand and a thrusting spear in his right. However, on his head he is here reconstructed wearing a Western Celtic helmet (derived from the Boeotian helmet) with a Montefortino-type crest knob, to which is attached a horsehair crest. His horse is again furnished with a simple pad saddle and blanket.

The third vignette (**3**) depicts a Gallic noble serving as a cavalryman with the army of Caesar during his campaigns in Gaul. He is wearing a mail shirt over a tunic and arming garment. He carries a flat, oval shield characteristic of his people in his left hand and a thrusting spear in his right. On his head he wears a Port helmet. His horse has a four-horned saddle over a blanket with ring-junctioned harness. As such, he presages the equipment of the cavalrymen of the Early Principate.

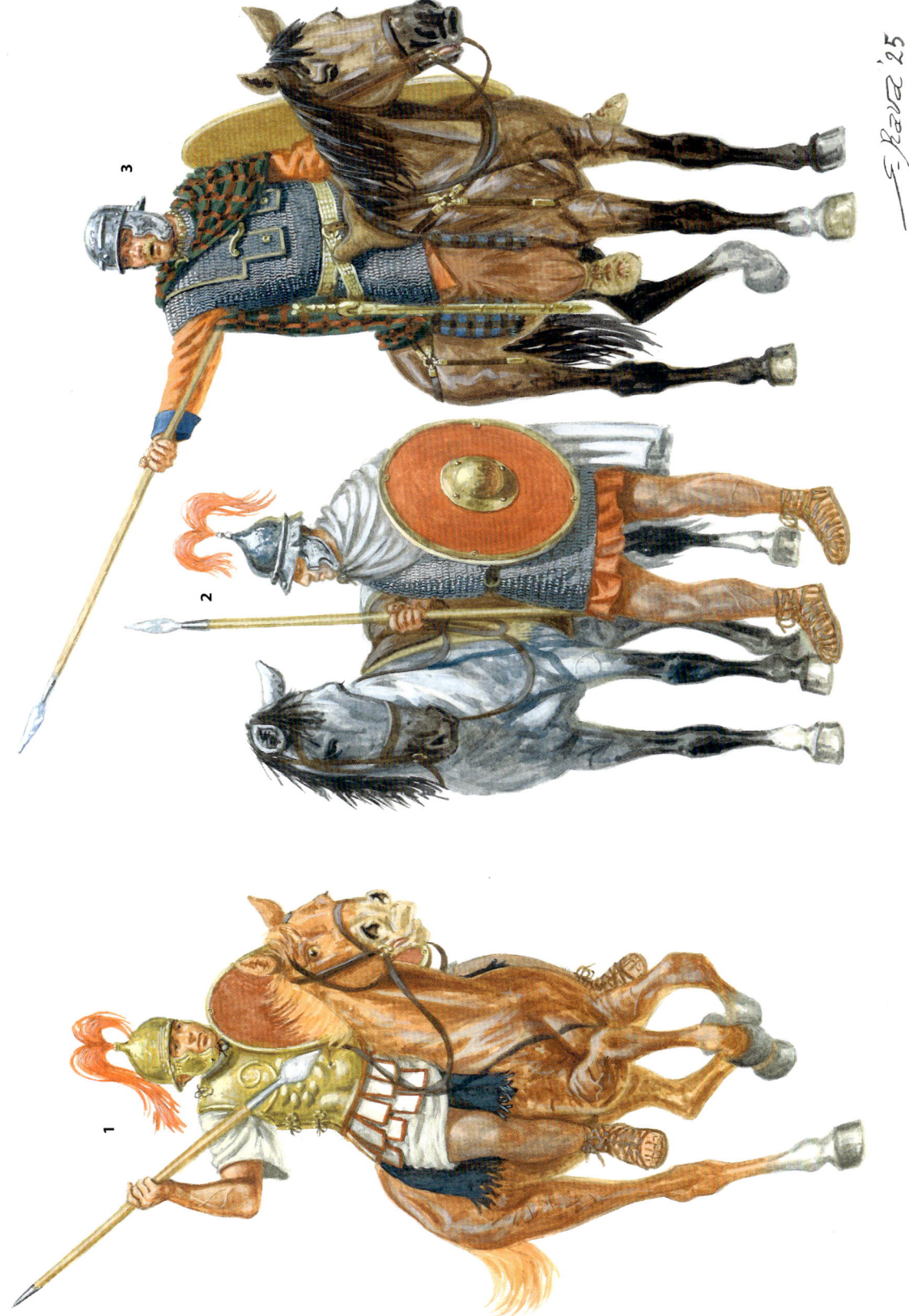

increase in size from the Early to Late Principate. This was probably due to the fact that cavalrymen did not experience a serious threat to the back of the neck and top of the shoulders in the same way that infantrymen did.

Next is the absence of a brow guard, a feature introduced to infantry helmets at the beginning of the Early Principate. This suggests that the problem such an addition was designed to counter – a downward blow to the face endangering the nose of the wearer – likewise did not occur for mounted troops.

Similarly, cavalry helmets did not incorporate the cross-piece reinforces that became common on infantry helmets during the High Principate. Again, this indicates that the need for such enhancements was not a consideration in cavalry combat, inevitably a result of the way in which Roman cavalry were used.

Finally, cavalry helmet cheek pieces almost invariably covered the rider's ear, often bearing moulded detail mimicking the human ear. The reason for this at first glance seems unclear, but it was perhaps enabled by the fact that cavalrymen did not rely on vocal commands but rather followed visual commands from movements of the standards combined with aural instructions from musical instruments, much easier to hear in battle (or even just over the sound of horses moving) than the human voice. The helmets of infantrymen, by contrast, for the most part left the ears exposed and even protected them where they protruded from the helmet bowl with dedicated ear guards.

Although face-mask helmets were not used in combat, they arguably had an important role in training for battle. Their primary function was to protect the heads of those riders who acted as targets during the *hippika gymnasia*, just as chamfrons and eye guards protected the heads of their horses. Even though only dummy javelins were used in this form of training, they could still maim in certain circumstances, hence the need for facial protection.

A secondary function of face-mask helmets may have been much more sophisticated, however. The masks themselves were normally equipped with an aperture for the mouth, one for each of the nostrils and one for each eye.

The Lacus Curtius relief, an Early Principate copy of a Republican original. (Photo © M.C. Bishop)

As with battle helmets, there were no ear openings. Experiment has shown how the mouth and nostril openings could limit the amount of air taken in, and the eye openings definitely restricted the field of view of a wearer, with a trade-off between vision and breathing dependent upon the fit of the mask (Petitjean *et al.* 2019: 220–21). This would undoubtedly affect the situational awareness of a rider wearing such a helmet, increasing his vulnerability, and would inevitably encourage the individual concerned to scan his surroundings by means of head movements more than he might if there was no mask. As a cavalryman's eyes were slightly behind the apertures (by how much is uncertain, because no examples of masks with lining or padding intact have survived), the edges of the apertures limited the field of view in both the vertical and horizontal axes. The importance of field of view to individuals is well known (Sim & Kaminski 2012: 81, Figs 49–50) and has been studied: in extreme cases, restricting it can lead to disorientation, as well as dizziness, unsteadiness and even bodily discomfort (Alfano & Michel 1990).

Modified face-mask helmet from Thorsberg Moor. (Einsamer Schütze/Wikimedia/ CC BY-SA 3.0)

An unusual visor helmet from a watery deposit at Thorsberg Moor may be relevant here (Matešić 2016). Although it is often seen in the context of helmets with visors, like the pseudo-Corinthian or Pfrondorf types, the unique shape of the cut-out and the surviving chin and underside of the lower lip of the face suggest that this is in fact an adaptation of a regular face-mask helmet. Its presence beyond the empire, whether as booty or a traded item, suggests that it was not ultimately used in its intended fashion. Indeed, the cut-out may have been made precisely because it was wished to use it in combat and, in order to do so, its most limiting feature had to be removed.

The role-playing aspect of the *hippika gymnasia*, indicated by the Greek/ Amazon/Trojan masks from the late 2nd/early 3rd centuries AD, as well as earlier mythological themes of many helmets (Hunter, pers. comm.) is an interesting aspect of the whole process of the use of masks. Appropriately enough, the word for a mask in Latin was *persona* and it seems indicative of the incorporation of a storytelling component from the beginning. Arrian, however, makes no mention of role playing in his treatise. One reason for the adoption of the Trojan War theme, suggested by some writers, may be an identification with the *lusus Troiae*, the aristocratic equestrian ritual revived by Julius Caesar, according to Suetonius (*Divus Iulius* 23.6), in which teams of young riders undertook a series of mounted evolutions. It was described by Vergil (*Aeneid* 5.580–87) in the context of the early days of Rome, although written in the Augustan period.

CARRIAGE

Cavalry helmets never seem to have been fitted with carrying handles, in contrast to their infantry counterparts. This suggests that they were not carried or stowed in the same ways when not actually being worn. Just as now, a helmet would have been advantageous to a rider in the event of a fall, and even the best cavalryman could be unseated if his horse was felled beneath him. Nevertheless, not all cavalrymen are shown wearing helmets on figural tombstones. Vonatorix of *ala Longiniana* is depicted bareheaded, but it is likely that this was through a desire not to obscure the head of the deceased, rather than an accurate portrayal of standard practice.

Ties

Montefortino helmets employed a three-point fastening system, using rings hinged to the underside of the neck guard, to carry one long lace that was then tied under the chin. Surviving Boeotian helmets lacked such an arrangement, however, so an alternative system must have been employed. Although it is possible to reconstruct a single-lace method of using holes in some helmets to provide a means of tying the helmet under the chin (Conyard 2018: 200), not all Boeotian helmets possessed these. In contrast, Western Celtic helmets used the three-point fastening system – perhaps another point in favour of identifying them as Roman.

Weyler-type helmets were fastened by means of the standard Roman three-point system, using rings attached to the centre of the underside of the neck guard and the inside (near the bottom) of each cheek piece. No examples have survived, but it is assumed that a single leather lace was passed through all three rings and then tied under the chin with a bow (a detail omitted in tombstone reliefs). The same will have been true for most pseudo-Attic battle helmets, as they possessed cheek pieces, but the Worthing helmet and visor points the way to a different way of securing a helmet to the head.

Face-mask helmets were hinged at the top of the mask and then secured in place by means of two studs, one in each of the exterior lower corners of the mask itself, with a leather strap passing around the back of the helmet, in the occipital region just above the neck guard. It is this system that was adopted for the hybrid Worthing bowl and visor, for obvious reasons.

Relief from Arlon showing cavalrymen in action wearing Weyler-type helmets. (FrDr/Wikimedia/CC BY-SA 4.0)

The stud presumably passed through a slit in the leather, although whether this was reinforced in any way is unknown, as it would doubtless have been prone to splitting otherwise. An alternative method would have been to use a buckle on the strap, as has been proposed for visor helmets like that from Heddernheim (Robinson 1975: Fig.130).

Ridge helmets differed from those of the Principate in that the neck guard was movable and a three-point fastening system was less practicable. One solution employed with a reconstruction of the Peel helmet was to employ a two-point system and just provide tie loops on the inside of the cheek pieces to be knotted under the chin (Dolmans 2018: 242).

Lining

All helmets needed lining and, most particularly, padding to function effectively: it provided a secure fit for the wearer and served to absorb some of the shock of a blow to the helmet. For the Principate, it is rare to find traces surviving, as it was invariably organic and prone to decay with time after burial. Nevertheless, the lining must have incorporated padding, particularly if it was intended that face masks should be close-fitting (and help dissipate any impact during the casting of missiles as part of the *hippika gymnasia*). Principate linings were probably glued in place, but Dominate helmets normally possessed evenly spaced holes around the edges of the bowl, cheek pieces and neck guard that were intended for stitching to attach its organic lining, probably leather. A reconstruction of the Peel helmet suggested that the lining had to be in place before the cheek-piece and neck-guard hinges could be attached to the bowl (Dolmans 2018: 242).

As Vegetius noted, cavalrymen during the Dominate wore a flat-topped cap, the *pilleus Pannonicus*, which could have served as additional padded lining when wearing a helmet: 'Up until now, the custom has persisted that all soldiers wore caps, which they called "Pannonian", fashioned from animal skins; this was done so that a heavy helmet would not seem burdensome in battle to a man who was always wearing something on his head' (Vegetius, *DRM* 1.20, tr. author).

Relief from the palace at Gamzigrad depicting a cavalryman wearing a 'pillbox' cap, usually identified as a *pileus Pannonicus*. (Institute for the Study of the Ancient World/ Flickr/CC BY 2.0)

It has long been thought that the appearance of the *pilleus Pannonicus* is known from iconographic sources like the statue of the two pairs of embracing tetrarchs (Diocletian and Galerius in the East, Maximian and Constantius in the West) incorporated into the fabric of St Mark's Basilica in Venice (Italy), known to have been looted from Constantinople. Doubt has been cast upon this interpretation (Džamtovski 2018), but its 'pillbox' form can also be seen on a relief from Gamzigrad (Serbia), being worn by a helmetless mounted man.

Unlike infantry helmets (Bishop 2025: 55), the evidence that cavalry helmets were provided with covers for protection when not in use is non-existent, although it is not an unreasonable assumption. This would particularly be the case for face-mask helmets, which cannot have seen frequent use, especially during the campaigning season.

OWNERSHIP

Being rich enough to afford to own and maintain a horse, along with the necessary equipment that went with it, let alone the panoply of the rider himself, meant that cavalry had long been the domain of social elites in the ancient world. Augustus revolutionized this system by enabling ordinary provincials, *peregrini* as they were known, to serve in the cavalry, with the promise of full Roman citizenship for them and their descendants, should they survive. The solution he came up with was ingenious: every time soldiers were paid, small deductions (usually recorded as '*arma*' in contemporary documentation) were made, so that *equites* effectively paid for their equipment on hire purchase. It was evidently soon realized that these assets could be exploited, with a loan document indicating their use as collateral on loans: a cavalryman used his silvered helmet and *insignia* and silver dagger scabbard to borrow 400 *drachmae* from an infantryman in a cohort (*P. Vindob.* L135).

Because soldiers owned their equipment – special dispensation, the *peculium militare*, had to be made under Roman law so that they, rather than their fathers, actually owned it – they were naturally keen to leave their mark wherever possible. This came in the form of terse little inscriptions, usually punched with a point (*punctim*) but occasionally scratched, typically in the form of the name of the *decurio* and the name of the owner, the classic means of identifying oneself within a unit.

Ownership inscriptions on the Theilenhofen helmet:
(**1**) ALIQ[*u*]ANDI; (**2**) COH[*ors*] III BRAGAR[*ugustanorum*];
(**3**) T[*urma*] NONI ('formerly from the *turma* of Nonus, in *cohors III Bracaraugustanorum*').
(Drawings © M.C. Bishop)

1

2

3

Such inscriptions are of course prevalent on both cavalry battle and face-mask helmets. The pseudo-Attic battle helmet from Theilenhofen (Germany) names troopers (and the *decuriones* under whom they served) in *cohors III Bracaraugustanorum* in both *punctim* and graffito style ('Atto in the *turma* of Paterclus' and 'Flavius Flavianus in the *turma* of Ataulvanus', both of them *equites*, not officers). The Ribchester face-mask helmet bears a *punctim* inscription CARAVI ('belonging to Caravus'), while the bowl of a face-mask helmet from Newstead is inscribed VFFI T GES (probably 'belonging to Uffus, in the *turma* of Ges...'). A face mask from the Straubing hoard (Germany) bears two *punctim* texts, T MAX QVINTI ('[from the] *turma* of Max[imus], the helmet of Quintus') and T MAX INGENVI ('[from the] *turma* of Max[imus], the helmet of Ingenuus'), suggesting that the helmet passed between two members of the same *turma* of their unit (probably the *cohors I Flavia Canathenorum milliaria sagittariorum*), perhaps as a purchase or even a bequest.

The inscription on the Berkasovo 1 ridge helmet (see p.37) not only mentions the owner (Dizzon) and the craftsman who made it (Avitus), but uses a formula (in Greek) 'use with good health' that echoes the common Latin phrase *utere felix* found on contemporary (and earlier) Roman military equipment (Bishop & Coulston 2006: 219). The inscription on Berkasovo 2 reads '*Vicit[...]iciniana*', possibly referring to the owner and the name of his unit ([Lic]iniana?). The provenance of these helmets is close to the border between the Latin-speaking Western Empire and the Greek-speaking East, so it is unsurprising that both Latin and Greek texts appear.

As was the case for Roman infantry (Bishop 2025: 4), a cavalryman's helmet was one of the most important parts of his equipment and discarding it deliberately was forbidden under military law:

> It is a serious crime for a soldier to sell his arms, and it is considered equal to that of desertion where he disposes of all of them; however, if he only sells a portion, his punishment will depend upon what he sold. For if he sells the armour for his legs or shoulders, he shall be punished by scourging; if, however, he sells his breastplate [*lorica*], his shield [*scutum*], his helmet [*galea*], and his sword [*gladius*], it is as if he is a deserter. (Justinian, *Digest* 49.16.14.1, citing Paulus, *On Military Punishments*)

WHO WORE WHAT?

The two helmets from the *cohors equitata* fort of Theilenhofen serve to make the point that, for most of the Principate, cavalry and infantry helmets differed considerably. No concession to such differentiation was made in the reliefs on the helical frieze of Trajan's Column, however, on which nearly all auxiliary troops, whether infantry or cavalry, are shown wearing generic derivatives of Attic helmets with a characteristic apex ring (as yet not manifested archaeologically among known cavalry helmets).

One of the more persistent notions about face-mask helmets is that they were worn by infantry *signiferi* (standard bearers). The origin of this lies with two tombstones of legionary *signiferi* from Mainz, one quite clearly a copy of the other (although which came first is not easy to tell). Gaius Valerius Secundus and Quintus Luccius Faustus, both of *legio XIV Gemina*, have stylized helmets above their left shoulders (so in the top right of the figural area). Within these helmets are crude representations of eye and mouth apertures and this has led to the suggestion that they are intended to represent face masks. This has been further reinforced, it seems, by the discovery of a face mask among the finds related to the battlefield site at Kalkriese, usually now associated with the Varan disaster of AD 9. The level of detail on the sculptures, however, in both instances, does not match that on the faces of the deceased individuals, so it is at the very least questionable whether such an identification is plausible, not least as sculptors had no difficulty in representing a face mask on a near-contemporary *congeries armorum* relief from Arlon (Belgium). So, if not face masks, what are these? It is possible that they represent the equivalent of early modern wig stands upon which the helmets were placed for display purposes. Moreover, if face-mask helmets were indeed used by infantry *signiferi*, it is odd that Arrian does not mention this in his description of the use of such headgear in the *hippika gymnasia* (see p.50).

Face mask from the Varusschlacht site at Kalkriese. (Carole Raddato/Wikimedia/ CC BY-SA 2.0)

A similar idea is that cavalrymen were depicted on tombstones wearing face-mask helmets. This has certainly been suggested in the case of the Reiter tombstone of Flavinus from the *ala Petriana* (see p.14). This is highly unlikely where cheek pieces can be discerned, however, because only one out of all of the face-mask helmets so far found – that from Vize (Turkey) – depicts cheek pieces on the face mask itself. Moreover, as noted above (see p.50), only selected riders wore face-mask helmets in the *hippika gymnasia*, and the coincidence of having only found tombstones belonging to such men stretches credulity.

Despite Hadrian's rather patronizing comments in the Lambaesis inscription (Speidel 2006: Field 30) about the inferiority of *equites* in *cohortes equitatae* to those in *alae*, whether it be in performance, pay or equipment, it is perhaps ironic that some of the finest face-mask helmets come from the 3rd-century AD hoard recovered from near the fort at Straubing, which was garrisoned by a *cohors equitata*.

Helmets of both auxiliary cavalry (left) and infantry (right) depicted on Trajan's Column. (Photos © M.C. Bishop)

Comparison of the tombstone reliefs of *legio XIIII Gemina signiferi* G. Valerius Secundus (left) and Q. Luccius Faustus (right) depicting what have been interpreted as face-mask helmets. (Photos © M.C. Bishop)

LEGACY

Face mask helmet from Vize, the only example imitating cheek pieces. (Photo © Dan Diffendale)

Of all the Roman helmet types, infantry or cavalry, the type with the strongest claim to a legacy is the cavalry ridge helmet from the Dominate. It shares this with the *spatha*, the Roman long sword that exerted a similar influence over early medieval blades in north-western Europe (Bishop 2020: 70–74). Its influence can be seen in many of the early medieval helmets of north-western Europe, notably Saxon and Viking pieces. Helmets like the Coppergate, Benty Grange and even Sutton Hoo (all England) examples, are included within this category (James 1986: 134). They shared the multipartite construction, separate neck guard, nasal and (in some cases) the large cheek pieces of the Late Roman cavalry helmets. Indeed, it has been noted that the Coppergate helmet had more in common with its Late Roman predecessors than it did with other contemporary helmets (Tweddle 1992: 1122). Similarly, the Benty Grange helmet has a cross on its nasal, reminiscent of the Chi-Rho found on the Alsóhetény helmet (see p.46). Whether there was a conscious effort to mimic known examples of ridge helmets is unknown (and probably unknowable), although it has been mooted that the crest on the Staffordshire Hoard (England) helmet could have been influenced by Roman helmets (Cooper 2021). Nevertheless, the mechanism for how such mimicry came to be so is as opaque as that which saw the Sassanian helmet type found in the mine at Dura-Europos evolve into the ridge helmets of the Dominate.

Reconstruction of the Anglo-Saxon helmet from Sutton Hoo, made of tinned copper-alloy plates covering a ferrous core. (Photo © M.C. Bishop)

BIBLIOGRAPHY

ANCIENT SOURCES

AE – L'Année Epigraphique. Available from Epigraphik-Datenbank Clauss/Slaby at https://db.edcs.eu/epigr/epi.php?s_sprache=en

Ammianus, *The History*. 1939–50 Loeb edition, trans. J.C. Rolfe. Available at https://penelope.uchicago.edu/Thayer/E/Roman/Texts/Ammian/home.html

Arrian, *Tēchnē taktike*. Available at https://el.wikisource.org/wiki/%CE%A4%CE%AD%CF%87%CE%BD%CE%B7_%CE%A4%CE%B1%CE%BA%CF%84%CE%B9%CE%BA%CE%AE

Isidore of Seville, *Etymologiae*. Available at https://penelope.uchicago.edu/Thayer/E/Roman/Texts/Isidore/home.html

Justinian, *Digest*. 1932 Central Trust Company edition, trans. S.P. Scott. Available at https://constitution.org/2-Authors/sps/sps11.htm

Lucian of Samosata, *Macrobioi*. Available at https://www.attalus.org/translate/macrobii.html

Polybios, *Histories*. 1922–27 Loeb edition, trans. W.R. Paton. Available at ttps://penelope.uchicago.edu/Thayer/E/Roman/Texts/Polybius/home.html

Suetonius, *The Twelve Caesars*. Available at https://penelope.uchicago.edu/thayer/e/roman/texts/suetonius/12caesars/home.html

Tacitus, *Germania*. 1876, trans. A.J. Church & W.J. Brodribb. Available at https://en.wikisource.org/wiki/Germania

Theoderet, *Ecclesiastical History*. Available at https://www.newadvent.org/fathers/27021.htm

Theodosianus, Codex. Available at https://droitromain.univ-grenoble-alpes.fr/Codex_Theod.htm

Vegetius, *De Re Militari*. 1885 Lang edition. Available at https://www.thelatinlibrary.com/vegetius.html

Vergil, *Aeneid*. Available at https://www.perseus.tufts.edu/hopper/text?doc=Perseus:text:1999.02.0054

Xenophon, *Peri hippikēs*. Available at https://www.perseus.tufts.edu/hopper/text?doc=Perseus%3Atext%3A1999.01.0210%3Atext%3DHorse

MODERN SOURCES

Abdul-Hak, S. (1954–55). 'Rapport préliminaire sur des objets provenant de la nécropole romaine située a proximité de Nawa (Hauran)', *Les Annales Archéologiques de Syrie* 4–5: 163–88.

Alfano, P.L. & Michel, G.F. (1990). 'Restricting the field of view: perceptual and performance effects', *Perceptual and Motor Skills* 70: 35–45.

Bishop, M.C. (1990). 'On parade: status, display, and morale in the Roman army', in Vetters, H. & Kandler, M., eds, *Limes XIV*, Vienna: ÖAW: 21–30.

Bishop, M.C. (2020). *The Spatha: The Roman Long Sword*. Weapon 72. Oxford: Osprey.

Bishop, M.C. (2022). *Roman Plate Armour*. Elite 247. Oxford: Osprey.

Bishop, M.C. (2025). *Roman Infantry Helmets*. Elite 266. Oxford: Osprey.

Bishop, M.C. & Coulston, J.C.N. (2006). *Roman Military Equipment from the Punic Wars to the Fall of Rome*, 2nd Edition. Oxford: Oxbow Books.

Bottini, A., *et al.* (1988). *Antike Helme*. Mainz: RGZM.

Breeze, D.J., ed. (2018). *The Crosby Garrett Helmet*. Kendal: CWAAS.

Breeze, D.J. & Bishop, M.C., eds (2013). *The Crosby Garrett Helmet*. Pewsey: Armatura.

Conyard, J. (2018). 'Reconstructing Classical Greek cavalry', in Coulston, J.C.N., ed., *Cavalry in the Roman World*. Pewsey: Armatura: 195–205.

Cooper, F. (2021). 'Anglo-Saxon bling – a warrior king's golden helmet', *Gold Bulletin* https://doi.org/10.1007/s13404-021-00297-2

Couissin, P. (1926). *Les Armes Romaines*. Paris: Champion.

Curle, J. (1911). *A Roman Frontier Post and its People. The Fort at Newstead in the Parish of Melrose*. Glasgow: Maclehose.

Dautova-Ruševljan, V. and Vujović, M. (2011). *Kasnoantički šlem iz Jarka / Late Roman Helmet from Jarak*. Novi Sad: Museum of Vojvodina.

Dittmann, K.H. (1940). 'Ein eiserner Spangenhelm in Kairo', *Germania* 24: 54–58.

Dolmans, M. (2018). 'Deurne revisited: the construction and "hypothetical" reconstruction of a Late Roman cavalry helmet', in Coulston, J.C.N., ed., *Cavalry in the Roman World*, *JRMES* 19: 227–46.

Džamtovski, M. (2018). 'Late Antique cylindrical hats as markers of authority and prestige', *JRMES* 20: 87–101.

Fairon, G. & Moreau-Maréchal, J. (1983a). 'La tombe au casque de Weiler, commune d'Autelbas, près d'Arlon', *Germania* 61: 551–64.

Fairon, G. & Moreau-Maréchal, J. (1983b). 'La tombe au casque de Weyler (commune d'Autelbas), près d'Arlon', *Bulletin trimestriel de l'institut archéologique du Luxembourg Arlon* 59: 1–2, 3–20.

Feugère, M. (1994). *Les casques antiques*. Paris: Editions Errance.

Fischer, T. (2018). 'Zu römischen Kavalleriehelmen der frühen und mittleren Kaiserzeit', in Pauli Jensen, X. & Grane, T., eds, *Imitation and Inspiration*, *JRMES* 17: 101–12.

Fischer, T. (2019). *Army of the Roman Emperors*. Oxford: Oxbow.

Frere, S.S. & St Joseph, K.K. (1974). 'The Roman fortress at Longthorpe', *Britannia* 5: 1–129.

Hoss, S. & Verstegen, U. (2025). 'Early Christian themes and symbols on Roman militaria of the 4th to 6th/7th Centuries CE', *Frontières* [Online], Supplément 3. Available at http://journals.openedition.org/frontieres/4277

James, S. (1986). 'Evidence from Dura-Europos for the origins of Late Roman helmets', *Syria* 63: 107–34.

James, S.T. (2014). 'The Boston helmet: a preliminary account of a Parthian/Roman-era artefact in the Museum of Fine Arts', in Collins, R. & McIntosh, F., eds, *Life in the Limes*, Oxford: Oxbow: 96–104.

Kaminski, J & Sim, D. (2014). 'The production and deposition of the Witcham Gravel Helmet',

Proceedings of the Cambridge Antiquarian Society 103: 69–82.

Kaminski, J. & Sim, D.N. (2019). 'Interpreting the Ribchester Helmet', *Arms & Armour* 16:1: 1–26.

Keim, J. & Klumbach, H. (1976). *Der römische Schatzfund von Straubing*. München: Beck.

Klumbach, H. (1973). *Spätrömische Gardehelme*. München: Beck.

Klumbach, H. (1974). *Römische Helme aus Niedergermanien*. Köln: Rheinland-Verlag.

Lindenschmit, L. (1881). *Die Alterthümer unserer heidnischen Vorzeit*, Bd 3. Mainz: von Zabern.

Lindenschmit, L. (1900). *Die Alterthümer unserer heidnischen Vorzeit*, Bd 4. Mainz: von Zabern.

Matešić, S. (2016). 'Ein germanischer Helm aus dem Thorsberger Moor', in Voss, H.-U. & Müller-Scheessel, N., eds, *Archäologie zwischen Römern und Barbaren*. Bonn: Habelt: 663–82.

Meijers, R. & Willer, F., eds (2007). *Achter het zilveren masker. Hinter der silbernen Maske*. Nijmegen: Museum het Valkhof.

Miks, C. (2014). *Ein spätrömischer Depotfund aus Koblenz am Rhein*. Mainz: RGZM.

Mitschke, S. (2007). 'De organische bekleding op de riuterhelmen uit Nijmegen en Xantel-Ward', in Meijers, R. & Willer, F., eds (2007). *Achter het zilveren masker. Hinter der silbernen Maske*. Nijmegen: Museum het Valkhof: 81 100.

Negin, A. (2015). 'Roman helmets with a browband shaped as a vertical fronton', *Historia i Świat* 4: 31–46.

Paddock, J.M. (1993). *The Bronze Italian Helmet from the Last Quarter of the Sixth Century B.C. to the Third Quarter of the First Century A.D.* PhD thesis, University of London.

Pernet, L. (2010). *Armement et auxiliaires gaulois*. Montagnac: éditions Monique Mergoil.

Petitjean, M., Bishop, M.C. & Griffiths, W.B. (2019). 'Experimenting with Roman cavalry: the *Hadrian's Cavalry Turma!* project', *JMRES* 19: 217–26.

Rațiu, A., *et al.* (2023). 'The Roman sports cavalry helmet from Islaz (Teleorman County, Romania)', *Cercetări Arheologice* 30.2: 669–90.

Robinson, H.R. (1975). *The Armour of Imperial Rome*. London: Arms & Armour.

Robinson, H.R. & Embleton, R. (1978). *What the Soldiers Wore on Hadrian's Wall*. Newcastle upon Tyne: Frank Graham.

Schaaff, U. (1988). 'Keltische Helme', in Bottini *et al.* 1988: 293–326.

Schalles, H.-J. & Schreiter, C. (1993). *Geschichte aus dem Kies. Neue Funde aus dem Alten Rhein bei Xanten*, Xantener Berichte 3. Köln: Rheinland-Verlag.

Score, V., ed. (2011). *Hoards, Hounds and Helmets*. Leicester: ULAS.

Sharp, H. (2021). 'The Hallaton Helmet and militaria – 20 year review'. *TLAHS* 95: 23–66.

Sharp, H. (2024). 'Roman replicas: recreating the Hallaton helmet', *Current Archaeology* 415: 38–43.

Sim, D. & Kaminski, J. (2012). *Roman Imperial Armour*. Oxford: Oxbow Books.

Sim, D.N. & Kaminski, J. (2017). 'The production and deposition of the Guisborough Helmet', *Arms & Armour* 14:1: 1–33.

Speidel, M.P. (2006). *Emperor Hadrian's Speeches to the African Army*. Mainz: RGZM.

Stoyanov, T., *et al.* (2023). 'Investigation of a Boeotian type helmet from the Regional Museum of History – Ruse', *Archaeologia (Sofia)* 1–2: 26–36.

Taylor, M.J. (2017). 'Etruscan identity and service in the Roman army: 300–100 B.C.E.', *American Journal of Archaeology* 121:2: 275–92.

Toynbee, J.M.C. & Clarke, R.R. (1948). 'A Roman decorated helmet and other objects from Norfolk', *Journal of Roman Studies* 38:1–2: 20–27.

Tweddle, D. (1992). *The Anglian Helmet from 16–22 Coppergate*. London: YAT/CBA.

Waurick, G. (1988a). 'Helme der hellenistischen Zeit und ihre Vorläufer', in Bottini *et al.* 1988: 151–80.

Waurick, G. (1988b). 'Römische Helme', in Bottini *et al.* 1988: 327–538.

Willems, W.J. (1994). 'Roman cavalry helmets in ritual hoards from the Kops Plateau at Nijmegen, The Netherlands', *JRMES* 5: 125–37.

INDEX

References to illustrations are shown in **bold**. Plates are shown with page locators in parentheses.